"As a therapist, I have found anger to be one of the most complicated, confusing emotions that people have, yet few resources deal with this topic. *Instant Anger Management* provides a comprehensive and easy-to-understand guide to coping with anger, including why we get angry and how to handle anger without becoming destructive. People will like the 'try this' sections, which clearly describe strategies to manage anger and stay emotionally healthy."

—**Marisol Hanley, PhD**, psychologist, and partner at
Seattle Psychology PLLC

"A much-needed resource, this book makes anger management easily accessible and relatable. This book is a must-have for therapists helping clients identify go-to strategies that truly work in diffusing anger. Beyond therapists, I highly recommend this book as a must-read; anyone can benefit from having tools in dealing with anger. Aaron has made anger management straightforward and simple!"

—**Melissa A. Frey, LCSW**, therapist, and owner
of Frey & Associates

T0001389

"Karmin's book normalizes the experience of anger and empowers the reader—through easily accessed tools—to shift their relationship to anger, rather than needing to eradicate those feelings entirely. Through his wise guidance and many years as a skilled therapist, Karmin offers readers an inner transformation, leading to increased resilience and self-control. Highly practical and incredibly insightful, this book can help ground you, guide you, and help you grow."

—**Cori Dixon-Fyle, LCSW**, founder and psychotherapist at Thriving Path, a counseling practice in Chicago, IL

"Aaron's second book gets right down to the techniques readers will need. He teaches readers how to question the assumptions fueling anger, and how to feel calmer and reinterpret the problem. He also looks at ways people can respond to someone else's anger. He teaches multiple ways to handle any situation so the reader can find a solution that works for them. It's a beginner-friendly guide in relatable language."

—**Aimee Daramus, PsyD**, licensed clinical psychologist specializing in mental illness, and author of *Understanding Bipolar Disorder*

"You won't find more bang for your buck in any self-help book on the market. Karmin uses his twenty years of clinical experience to effectively and decisively cut through the noise to deliver you this remarkably helpful text. This book is so jam-packed with (literally hundreds of) concrete things you can do to harness your anger today, that you may actually have difficulty closing it."

—**Nathan R. Hydes, PhD, ABPP**, board-certified
clinical psychologist

"I am so glad that Aaron Karmin wrote this book. In our busy, chaotic times, it is easy to let anger overcome us. This book provides straightforward, step-by-step guidance to help develop healthy skills to combat unhealthy anger and rage. I will be recommending this book to my clients with anger issues!"

—**Susan L. Bank, MD**, psychiatrist in private
practice in Chicago, IL

"Anger management is a skill that can be developed and can improve our lives personally, professionally, and financially. Aaron Karmin is a seasoned expert who makes anger management simple with clear tutorials, practical tips, and proven strategies from cognitive behavior therapy (CBT). This book is a wonderful resource, chock-full of wisdom that will help you quickly and easily improve your emotional intelligence and your life."

—**Joyce Marter, LCPC**, licensed psychotherapist, founder of Urban Balance, national public speaker, and author of *The Financial Mindset Fix*

Quick
and Simple
CBT Strategies
to Defuse Anger
on the Spot

INSTANT
ANGER
MANAGEMENT

AARON KARMIN, LCPC

New Harbinger Publications, Inc.

Publisher's Note

This publication is designed to provide accurate and authoritative information in regard to the subject matter covered. It is sold with the understanding that the publisher is not engaged in rendering psychological, financial, legal, or other professional services. If expert assistance or counseling is needed, the services of a competent professional should be sought.

In consideration of evolving American English usage standards, and reflecting a commitment to equity for all genders, 'they/them' is used in this book to denote singular persons.

Distributed in Canada by Raincoast Books

NEW HARBINGER PUBLICATIONS is a registered trademark of New Harbinger Publications, Inc.

Copyright © 2021 by Aaron Karmin

New Harbinger Publications, Inc.
5674 Shattuck Avenue
Oakland, CA 94609
www.newharbinger.com

Cover design by Sara Christian; Interior design by Amy Shoup and Michele Waters-Kermes; Acquired by Jess O'Brien; Edited by Brady Kahn

Library of Congress Cataloging-in-Publication Data

Names: Karmin, Aaron, author.
Title: Instant anger management : quick and simple cbt strategies to defuse anger on the spot / Aaron Karmin.
Description: Oakland : New Harbinger Publication, 2021.
Identifiers: LCCN 2021014192 | ISBN 9781684038398 (trade paperback)
Subjects: LCSH: Anger. | Cognitive therapy. | Self-help techniques.
Classification: LCC BF575.A5 K367 2021 | DDC 152.4/7--dc23
LC record available at https://lccn.loc.gov/2021014192

Printed in the United States of America

23   22   21

10   9   8   7   6   5   4   3   2   1   First Printing

CONTENTS

PART 4: **MAINTAINING A POSITIVE OUTLOOK**

PART 5: **EXPRESSING YOURSELF**

INTRODUCTION

IN TODAY'S WORLD, it's usually not the large things—the big, identifiable things—that lead to eruptions of hostility. It's the little, tiny things going on all the time that build up and cause anger. It's missing a parking place; it's the person in the grocery line with eleven items in their basket when they're only supposed to have ten. It's having the phone ring when we're trying to concentrate, or calling up somebody and then being left on hold, only to be disconnected. Here are more common examples of events or issues that can trigger anger:

- Long waits to see your doctor
- Traffic congestion
- Crowded buses
- A friend joking about a sensitive topic
- A friend not paying back money you loaned them
- Being falsely accused
- Having to clean up someone else's mess

- An untidy roommate

- A neighbor who plays music too loud

- Being given wrong directions

- Rumors being spread about you that are not true

- Having money or property stolen from you

Everyday events such as these can provoke our anger. Many times, specific events touch on sensitive areas in our life. These sensitive areas, like red flag warnings, usually relate to long-standing issues that can easily lead to anger.

While you may feel that you can do little to control your anger, there are things you can do to make a difference. This book aims to help you cope with anger. It includes techniques to help you begin to understand and deal with your anger in practical ways. Through this book, you will learn how to manage anger's impact on your body, mood, thoughts, and behavior in healthy ways. You will explore the purpose of anger and how to take responsibility for your choices. This book will help you identify situations that can quickly escalate your feelings of anger and provide you with skills to communicate more effectively.

PART 1

HOW ANGER WORKS

EVERYONE GETS ANGRY. Some people express their anger but then feel guilty about it. Others suppress angry feelings because they think anger is not nice. Others have difficulty expressing anger and get angry at themselves for not being able to express themselves. Some just lash out. Getting to know what triggers anger and how to react effectively can help us manage anger in a positive way.

Anger is an instinctual emotional response triggered by a real or imagined threat. Because anger is painful, we seek relief. Most people feel angry when someone or something obstructs them in some way. And many people respond to the feeling of anger by immediately wanting the satisfaction of forcing the obstacle out of the way—or, if it won't move, to curse and insult it. Anger management involves not saying or doing something that we will later regret. It involves calming ourselves, making a cool-headed assessment of the situation, and taking sensible action. To break the anger habit, we must develop an awareness of the events, circumstances, and behaviors of others that trigger our anger. This awareness also involves understanding the negative consequences that result from anger.

While everyone is born with the potential to feel and express anger, we each have our own learning experiences, which cause us to react to frustration differently. We learn from others, and one lesson we take away is to use our behavior rather than our words to convey emotions. Yet, the expression of anger does not have to involve yelling or violence; sadness does not have to involve crying; fear does not have to involve hiding or avoiding. There is no simple explanation for why some people are angrier than others; some of it might depend on our character or our early experiences. The following factors may contribute to our angry outbursts:

- **Habit**. Anger can become an automatic response to certain situations, and others may reinforce this habit if they have become used to us getting angry.

- **Fear**. Anger can be felt as a response to situations that we fear will overwhelm us if we do not go on the offensive.

- **Shame**. Anger can spring from the feeling that we have to fight to preserve our dignity and sense of self-worth.

- **Loss**. Anger commonly accompanies the sadness which goes with a bereavement or a severe setback.

- **Lack of assertiveness**. If we cannot speak up for ourselves and negotiate, we may find ourselves exploding instead.

- **Low frustration tolerance**. We go on the attack to deal with situations that most people would just put up with.

- **Response to past trauma**. If we have been badly hurt in the past, we may understandably react overly aggressive toward anything that seems threatening in the present.

By reflecting on these possible factors, we can become more aware of what triggers our anger. The pages ahead explore how the body responds to anger and the cues that arise when we are angry. This section will also discuss our thinking when mad and the consequences of internalizing anger.

1. Wired to Act Quickly

When we become angry, our body prepares itself for a crisis. We prepare for fight or flight. This is a hardwired and fast reaction in which the body gets literally ready to attack or to flee. For example, if a grizzly bear charged toward us, our body would need to do certain things for us to survive. People's hands get cold because the blood leaves the extremities, in case a bear might bite them off. This basically protects the body's blood supply and allows the blood to go to specific places to protect itself. In this automatic, instinctual routine, hormones pump rapidly through the body, the pupils dilate, the heart rate quickens, breathing becomes rapid and shallow, digestion slows down, sweat gland activity increases, and blood and oxygen drain from the brain into the larger muscles preparing them for rapid movement.

Notice the last part of the previous sentence: "and blood and oxygen drain from the brain..." This part is very important for understanding *why I do it* (get angry and yell). Stress, anger, fear: can all overwhelm the brain, depriving it of oxygen, which totally shuts down our ability to think. When this emotional flooding occurs, we cannot think straight. The term *flooding* describes the release of hormones that prepare our body for action. These chemicals must pass through our body, be absorbed into the tissues, and released into the urine before our body returns to normal. The flooding from the fight-or-flight process takes at least twenty minutes.

We will need a twenty-minute respite to completely calm down physiologically. If the stressful situation remains, our heart rate will remain elevated, our body will pump out adrenaline, and our thinking will be clouded. We will be physiologically reactive even if we know a different response is called for. Most people think they are calm long before they actually are physiologically calm.

This cranial takeover in our brain occurs because our logical prefrontal cortex is simply outmatched by the competition from our emotional amygdala. This race is not even close, because emotion-laden pathways in the brain are faster than logical signals. Our amygdala's emotional impulses zoom down our neurological express routes. While the same information is also being processed logically, our rational thoughts are transported via the local roads, stopping at other regions of our brain along the way. But because the emotional pathway in our brain transmits signals twice as fast as the more roundabout route involving logic, our judgment simply can't intervene in time. It takes time to think, plan, analyze, and act.

Our hunter-gatherer ancestors did not have the luxury of time. If they were confronted with a threat, they had to act immediately or they would die. They could not take a moment to weigh the pros and cons, analyze, and act: *Well, there is a bear in front of me. Do I look for honey? Shall I catch a salmon? Shape some wood into a spear? Grab a rock? Run away?* No, it was fight (attack) or flight (run away). It was not logical problem solving that helped them in that moment. Their emotional reactions allowed them to survive.

Is there nothing we can do? Are emotions outside our control? In one sense, yes. But in a more important sense, no! It is correct to say that emotions are an automatic physiological response. In that way, they are outside of our immediate control, like our eyes blinking. But we can become aware of our blinking, and similarly we can become mindful of what triggers our emotional reactions. If we can take control over our automatic reactions like blinking, breathing, and memory, it is also possible to take control of our emotional reactions.

2. Interpretation Matters

Our brain is adept at detecting a whole pattern from just a few clues. One result is that we are susceptible to *confirmation bias*, a type of selective thinking that causes us to notice evidence for what we already believe and to miss or discount evidence that might lead in another direction. When life unfailingly conforms to our most negative expectations, we can be sure that confirmation bias is at work.

This reminds me of a client I saw who had two failed marriages and concluded, "All women are after your money." From only two examples, he created a generalization that included billions of women! His anger, his unwillingness to allow any women to get close to him, was the side-effect of two fundamental facts about how the brain works: first, the brain has the amazing ability to see a pattern with minimal clues; and second, the brain has a tendency to look for evidence that confirms already existing beliefs. So once you have concluded something, you have a strong tendency to generalize that conclusion by noticing only evidence that supports your preexisting belief. Angry, cynical, or hostile feelings cause your mind to look for negative evidence and selectively ignore any positives. In this way the pain comes from making negative events larger and more awful than they really are.

When we feel anger or any other emotion, our response is the product of two factors: one, the objective physiological arousal that a particular event produces in us, and two, our subjective interpretation of the event. For example, if someone steps on our toe, we will feel pain, but our heart will also start beating faster. This reaction is automatic, and we have little control over our body's initial physical response. However, the emotions we experience are not automatic and will be influenced by our interpretation of the event. If we perceive that it was an accident and the person feels badly, we may feel compassion for the other person, even though we are in physical pain. If we perceive that it was on purpose, however, we may feel angry and that it shouldn't have happened.

Sometimes we interpret events as caused by situational factors (*I missed the flight because the traffic was bad*), whereas individuals with anger tend to attribute the same events to human factors (*I missed the flight because the cab driver was terrible*). This is because anger is typically caused by the actions of people and sadness by factors that are circumstantial. If we are overly sensitive to rejection, we may interpret meaningless interactions as a sign that someone is snubbing us. If we have a strict code of conduct, we may become angry whenever anyone bends the rules. We may interpret others' attempts to win a game as efforts toward superiority and dominance, so we assume they are putting us down and belittling us. Instead, try looking at anger in terms of the following interpretations:

1. **Seeking revenge**. We feel hurt, so we want to get even and make things fair.

2. **Preventing disaster**. We feel helpless, so we want to take control.

3. **Pushing others away**. We feel discouraged, so we want to withdraw from life and avoid being judged.

4. **Getting attention**. We feel disrespected, so we lash out to be acknowledged or to prove our importance.

5. **Expressing difficult feelings**. We are overwhelmed, so we want to reduce our discomfort.

If you find that you're often in a state of anger, you may want to examine the interpretations you're bringing to events, since your interpretations may be promoting angry thoughts that color your expectations about how your life will unfold. The key to our experience of emotion is our interpretation of events—not the events themselves.

3. Bottled Emotions

Most people are not taught how to fix these things called *emotions*. One lesson many of us are taught is to label some feelings (fear, sadness) as *bad* or negative states and others (anger, excitement) as *good* or positive. However, feelings are neither good nor bad; feelings just are. If we listen to our emotions and understand what they mean, we can address them, and their intensity will fade. But if we ignore what our emotions tell us, our feelings will build up and may result in a display of destructive behavior.

Emotions are part of our life and to deny them is to deny part of ourselves. I have seen people who have discussed painful experiences from fifteen to twenty years ago, saying "I thought I got over it. I guess I didn't!" Truthfully, they may have gotten over the initial experience, but the feeling is still as powerful as at when it was first formed. As a result, these emotions resurface and we reexperience the anger that was felt at some time in our past. Let's take a man who had a bad first marriage. He may relive an emotional experience of jealousy any time his wife mentions, "I might be late." The anger he feels when hearing this statement in the present triggers his brain to search for a memory and recall a feeling of jealousy from his first marriage. If the husband dwells on this feeling, he will become insecure, angry, and suspicious for no reason.

When an emotional memory is triggered, we will say the same things, feel the same intensity of emotion, and behave the same way we did at the time the memory was created. That is to say, we will respond to today as if it were a different time or place in our lives. As a result, we may become defensive and lash out with anger, or withdraw and avoid confrontation due to sadness or fear. Many of these reactions, however, are not appropriate for the current situation. These reactions are based on past relationships and emotional experiences that were never addressed.

4. Identify Your Cues

An important aspect of anger management is to identify the cues that occur in response to the anger-provoking event. These cues serve as warning signs that you have become angry and that your anger is continuing to escalate. They can be broken down into four cue categories: physical, behavioral, emotional, and cognitive (or thought) cues.

Physical cues involve the way our bodies respond when we become angry. For example, our heart rate may increase, we may feel tightness in our chest, or we may feel hot and flushed. These physical cues can also warn us that our anger is escalating out of control. We can learn to identify these cues when they occur in response to an anger-provoking event. Can you identify some of the physical cues that you have experienced when you have become angry?

- Faster heart rate

- Higher blood pressure

- Sweating

- Muscle tightness

- Headache

- Trembling or twitching

- Nausea or vomiting

- Sleep problems

- Fatigue

- Shallow breathing

Behavioral cues involve the behaviors we display when we get angry, which can be observed by other people around us. For example, we may clench our fists, pace back and forth, slam a door, or raise our voices. These behavioral responses are the second cue of our anger. What are some of the behavioral cues that you have experienced when you become angry?

- Kicking or throwing something

- Getting in someone's face

- Shoving, grabbing, hitting

- Breaking something

- Calling someone names

- Giving someone a dirty look

- Silent treatment

- Aggressive behaviors (like road rage)

- Increased alcohol or drug use

- Under- or overeating

- Reduced concentration

- Reduced motivation

- Accusations or blame

- Yelling

Emotional cues involve other feelings that may occur concurrently with our anger. For example, we may become angry when we feel abandoned, afraid, discounted, disrespected, guilty, humiliated, impatient, insecure, jealous, or rejected. These kinds of feelings are the core or primary feelings that underlie our anger. It is easy to discount these primary feelings, because they often make us feel vulnerable. An important component of anger management is to become aware of, and to recognize, the primary feelings that underlie our anger. We can view anger as a response to these underlying feelings. Can you identify some of the primary feelings you have experienced during an episode of anger?

- Hostility

- Sadness

- Guilt

- Jealousy

- Shock

- Worry

- Defensiveness

- Suspiciousness

- Shame

- Apathy (lack of interest)

- Panic

- Pessimism

Cognitive cues refer to the thoughts that occur in response to the anger-provoking event. These thoughts are based on how we interpret the event. For example, we may interpret a friend's comments as criticism, or we may interpret the actions of others as demeaning, humiliating, or controlling. Some people call these thoughts *self-talk,* because they resemble a conversation we are having with ourselves. When we are angry, this self-talk is usually very critical and hostile in tone and content. In turn, we expose our negative beliefs that the world is a bad place, based on unrealistic ideas about people, places, and things.

Closely related to thoughts and self-talk are fantasies and images. Fantasies and images are other types of cognitive cues that can indicate an escalation of anger. For example, we might fantasize about seeking revenge on a perceived enemy, or imagine or visualize our spouse having an affair. When we have these fantasies and images, our anger can escalate even more rapidly.

Here are some examples of cognitive or thought cues. Can you think of more?

- *They did that on purpose.*

- *They wanted to hurt me.*

- *They deserve this.*

- *They never even asked me.*

- *They're being unreasonable.*

- *You think you're better than me.*

- *I'll show you.*

- *It's not fair.*

- *They started it.*

- *They don't care about me.*

- *They cannot be trusted.*

When you're learning to manage your anger in a non-aggressive way, it is important to recognize how anger feels for you and get to know the situations that produce it. It's easier to take these first steps if you can become aware of your anger's characteristic physical, emotional, behavioral, and cognitive signs. Often, there are different signs in different situations or with different people in your life.

PART 2

TAKING CARE OF YOURSELF

WE EACH MAY HAVE FALLEN VICTIM to our daily routine becoming a series of tedious demands and unfulfilling obligations. Driving to our kid's soccer games, mowing the lawn, picking up the dry cleaning, visiting our mother-in-law, doing the dishes, taking the dog to the vet, cleaning the house, buying groceries... We are all bombarded every day with tasks, people, work, and obligations that make demands on our time and energy. It's easy to let these things overwhelm us and foster anger.

If you're overwhelmed and chronically angry, the logical, natural antidote to your stressful state is relaxation. After all, you can't be frustrated and relaxed at the same time—it's physiologically impossible. Relaxation is always within your reach because all it requires you to do is the things you do anyway: sleep, eat, and breathe.

Taking care of yourself will help maintain your physical, emotional, and mental reserves to prevent and manage anger. If you're so stressed that you feel like you don't have the time or energy to devote to self-care, that's when you need replenishment the most! Prioritizing self-care is a decision that only you can make, and changing behavior can take some effort.

This section explores self-care strategies to cope with feelings of anger. Doing some relaxation techniques for twenty minutes a day will enable you to respond calmly, rather than lashing out in anger. These skills help to calm your mind and body, which buffers the immediate impact that anger has on you.

5. Improving Sleep

You've probably heard the old saying "Never go to bed angry." Some say it goes back to the Bible, in Ephesians 4:26: "Let not the sun go down upon your wrath." But while resolving anger before bedtime is great advice, a more common problem is not getting enough sleep. Researchers suggest that when people are sleep deprived, they feel more irritable, angry, and hostile. In addition, sleep deprivation seems to be associated with more intense emotional reactivity, in that people who suffer from sleep loss are especially likely to react with anger when something doesn't go well for them.[1] This happens because sleep deprivation increases amygdala (emotional) activity and reduces prefrontal cortex (thinking) functioning in the brain. In other words: insomnia fuels increased anger and decreased judgment!

➡ TRY THIS

While there is merit to timely conflict resolution, sometimes it's actually better to go to bed angry than to stay up and get more fatigued. There is a strong chance that you will wake up in the morning not even thinking about the previous night's discussion. A small conflict that is not worth fighting over will be forgotten after a night of rest. If you are still upset in the morning, then you know you feel strongly about the issue. You can restart the discussion with a fresh perspective and a clear frame of mind, which will ultimately provide a better resolution. Here are some tips for better sleep habits.

Do not nap during the day. If we are having trouble sleeping at night, avoid naps during the day, because napping will throw off your body clock and make it even more difficult to sleep at night. If you are feeling especially tired, and feel as if you absolutely must nap, be sure to sleep for less than thirty minutes, and do it early in the day.

Limit caffeine and alcohol. Avoid drinking caffeine or alcohol several hours before bedtime. Although alcohol may initially act as a sedative, it can interrupt normal sleep patterns.

Don't smoke. Nicotine is a stimulant and can make it difficult to fall asleep and stay asleep. Many over-the-counter and prescription drugs may disrupt sleep as well.

Keep your bedroom peaceful and comfortable. Make sure the room is well ventilated and the temperature consistent, and try to keep it quiet. You could use a fan or a white-noise machine to help block outside sounds.

Hide your clock. A big illuminated digital clock may cause you to focus on the time and make you feel stressed and anxious. Place your clock so that you can't see the time when you are in bed.

If you are particularly angry, built-up stress can keep you up at night. It can come from any situation, but it will leave your heart racing and your mind stewing. In later chapters, you will learn how to let go of feelings of anger to help you get some sleep.

6. Eating Well

There is a connection between being hungry and feeling angry. How does this work? As humans, we have the choice to listen to our hunger or ignore it. Yet, in our busy and over-booked lives, we often choose to ignore this signal, waiting far too long to feed an empty stomach. Our body's response to being ignored is to cause an emotional reaction (like anger) to get our attention. And the longer we deprive ourselves, the greater the emotional response.

However, being *hangry* is dependent on context. If we're hungry and having a bad day and a coworker blames us for missing a deadline, we're likely to direct our anger at them. If we're hungry because we just ran through a field of daisies with a pack of adorable puppies, we might not be so snappy. Hunger signals to us that something is wrong—that it's time to eat. But as humans, we may interpret that aversive feeling as something external before we look into what our body is really telling us. This means that feeling hangry occurs when our hunger-induced negativity gets blamed on the external world around us. You think that the person who cut you off on the road is what made you angry—not the fact that you haven't eaten all day.

➡ TRY THIS

What can be done about hanger? To help manage your anger and satisfy your stomach, here are a few suggestions.

Make sure you always have some healthy food available. Trying to soothe hanger with candy or other junk food will just create a vicious cycle. The sugary snack will spike blood glucose for half an hour, but afterward you will crash again, as the insulin response removes the glucose from the bloodstream, once again alerting the brain to spring to action.

Don't skip meals. If you miss a meal, you miss the opportunity to provide energy to your mind and body. Waiting too long between times that you eat can create a drop in blood sugar, which could become seriously dangerous in some cases, causing lightheadedness or disorientation. You should not go more than four to five hours between meals, and for most of us, snacking between meals is essential.

Snack smart. The tried-and-true trio that will keep you going without blowing a fuse is a medley of protein, fat, and carbs. Whether it's a slice of cheese and whole grain crackers, cereal, or a homemade trail mix, be sure to keep these on-the-go snacks handy, so you have them readily available when you feel your mood diving toward a meltdown.

Fundamentally, learning to notice how hunger impacts your interpersonal reactions can create powerful opportunities for managing anger.

7. Breathing Deeply

Ever been told to take a deep breath when you feel angry? Well, it's good advice. That's because the first reaction to frustration is purely physiological: we receive a rush of adrenaline to prepare us to take action in real danger. In most cases, simply taking a few moments to practice deep breathing will allow our body to calm down.

When we deliberately take slow deep breaths, we are indirectly telling our body that all danger has now passed; as a consequence, our body will stop producing adrenaline and our arousal will cease. Slow deep breathing reverses our body's stress response of anger, slows the heart, reduces blood pressure, and releases endorphins, our body's natural painkillers.

You can try this. Place your hand on your stomach below your ribs. Begin by breathing in slowly through your nostrils like you were smelling a beautiful flower, or imagine that you are smelling the turkey on Thanksgiving or cookies baking on Christmas. Breathe in slowly and deeply, silently saying the word *in*.

Then pucker your lips and blow out. Imagine you are blowing on your cup of coffee to cool it off or as if you were blowing at a match, not enough to blow it out, just enough to make the flame flicker. Breathe out slowly and gradually, silently saying the word *out* as you let the air escape through pursed lips. You will feel your stomach move in and out against your hand. This is abdominal breathing or deep breathing—the kind of breathing we did naturally as babies and still do when we are asleep or very calm.

If it feels uncomfortable and you become dizzy or light-headed, slow your breathing down. If you take your pulse before and three minutes after deep breathing, you will find that your pulse has slowed down. That's right, you can control your heart rate simply by breathing this way.

➡ TRY THIS

··· BREATH ONE ···

Take a slow deep breath in through your nose

And breathe out slowly puckering your lips

As if you were blowing at a flame just enough to make it flicker

Don't attempt to force the air out, but just let the air flow out

Emptying all the air from your lungs

· · · BREATH TWO · · ·

Continue breathing in the nose like you're smelling perfume

Breathe out through your lips making a smooth stream of air

Smooth and gentle, calm and even, let the tension flow out

· · · BREATH THREE · · ·

Imagine that you are sniffing a very delicate flower

Let the flow of breath into your nose be smooth and gentle

And breathe out like you're blowing a cup of coffee

Making a stream of air that passes over your lips as you exhale

· · · BREATH FOUR · · ·

Sniff the air in through you nose like you're smelling cookies baking in the oven

Let yourself breathe out slowly and naturally, without effort

Breathe in and out, quietly and evenly at your own pace

Notice the refreshing and energizing air, as it quietly moves in and out of your lungs

Let the tension flow out with each breath

Breathing in strength and energy, breathing out tension and worry

Smooth and gentle, calm and even

Breathing in life and peace, breathing out tension and worry.

Start by practicing while in bed as you prepare for sleep. If you are able to perform relaxation breathing at times when you are not feeling angry, it will become easier to use in times of frustration. Similarly, when you really need to breathe deeply, you won't remember to do so unless you practice. Set aside some time to do deep breathing every day. As you become more adept, you may find yourself naturally moving into a deep-breathing mode whenever anger arises.

8. Mindfulness

Think of the last time you felt really angry. Your body may have been tense, your mind may have been dwelling on the past or anticipating problems in the future, and there was an intensity or urgency to take action immediately. For many people this urge to escape anger has developed into unhealthy strategies such as binge eating, shopping, sleeping, drinking, or other addictions.

Mindfulness can help us detach from anger-fueled circumstances and thoughts in a healthy way by redirecting our attention to what is happening in the present moment. It's basically a way to distract ourselves by focusing on something other than the difficult emotions we are experiencing. We may also think of mindfulness as grounding, centering, creating a safe place, or healthy detachment. Although mindfulness does not solve the problem that is contributing to our anger, it does provide a temporary way to gain control over our feelings and prevent things from getting worse.

Mindfulness anchors us, gives us a chance to calm down, and allows us to eventually return to and address the problem that is triggering anger to begin with. And mindfulness can be done anytime, anywhere, and no one has to know. Mindfulness encourages you to focus on some aspect of the physical world rather than on your internal thoughts and feelings of anger.

➡ TRY THIS

To experience mindfulness, designate a specific time for concentrating your full attention. Start initially for three minutes twice a day, and then gradually increase the frequency and duration. For example, when doing the dishes or taking a shower, you can practice using your senses to shift your focus and notice the following:

- The warmth of the water and how it feels on your skin

- The texture of the bubbles

- The light reflecting off the bubbles as they softly pop

- The slurp of the water as you move the dishes about

- The slipperiness of the dishes or soap

- The roughness of the sponge

- The fragrance of soap

You can incorporate other mindful meditation exercises into your daily life.

1. **Pick an activity** that is part of your morning routine, such as brushing your teeth, shaving, or having a shower. When you do it, totally focus on what you are doing moment by moment: the body movements, how things feel, taste, smell, look, sound, etc.

2. **Sitting at your desk**, grab the seat of your chair as hard as you can; notice the sensations in your fingers, palms, and wrists, the tightening of arm muscles as you hold on. Then quickly release your grip and take note of the sensations as they ebb. Is there a tingling in your palms? Allow your arms to completely relax, perhaps shaking them loosely by your sides, and notice the jiggling movement and air on your hands and any other sensations.

3. **Listen to music** with headphones to shut out external noise. Close your eyes and give yourself permission to listen only to the music.

4. **Choose a route**, preferably outdoors, where you can walk uninterrupted for at least twenty minutes. Remain connected with the sensations in your body and place your attention on the sights around you. You don't have to go slowly; just be aware of the moment-to-moment experience of walking.

5. **Sit in a comfortable chair** noticing the weight of your body as you settle in; wiggling your toes in your socks; feeling your back easing against the cushions.

6. **Stretch**. Extend your fingers, arms, and legs as far as you can; slowly and gently roll your head around.

7. **Eat something mindfully**. It could be a single grape or an entire meal. Eating mindfully means taking in the full experience as you bite in and chew, savor, and swallow. Describe the process, what you see and smell, the flavors, and the textures in detail to yourself.

Mindfulness teaches you how to be in the moment and focus on the here and now. In turn, you can recognize anger before it becomes explosive, before you lose control, so that you can release it and return quickly to a calm, rational state in which nonreactive and generally better decisions and communication can occur.

9. Journaling

One way to manage anger is to write your feelings down on a piece of paper. This technique may seem too easy to be of any use, yet it is very successful if you do it the right way, which means not writing a hate letter or a laundry list of complaints and criticisms. As you journal about your feelings, you are releasing your anger in a constructive way.

Writing involves making a choice and taking action in the real world. The power of choice is in itself a welcome antidote to the miserable feeling that there is nothing you can do about the pain your anger is causing you. The act of writing lends the feeling that there is something you can do about your anger, and you are doing it in the present. The power of choice is liberating, and writing gives you some timely relief from your own distress. If you are angry at a deceased loved one, at God, at life, at the system, or even at yourself, you can write your anger out of your heart and onto a piece of paper. Afterward you can file your letter, tear it up, or burn it. That is your choice too. Writing your painful feelings down on a piece of paper has the following effects:

- Makes them tangible and concrete before your very eyes. Abstract thoughts about your life or about yourself are impossible to manage, but you can begin to evaluate and sort them out when you see them in black-and-white in front of you.

- Helps to organize thoughts and give meaning to experiences.

- Enables you to regulate your emotions, which helps you break free of brooding or rumination.

- Begins a process of association that brings up ideas from the past that are inaccessible otherwise.

Writing may seem counterintuitive to many of us. Our anger can be so painful, and the thought of writing about experiences we wish to forget may cause fear that we will be overwhelmed. Yet, journaling helps to release our painful emotions. There is no way anyone can put a bandage on this hurt; our pain must be experienced, so we can heal and move on with our life. Writing gives us control over how and when these feelings come to the surface. And they will surface sooner or later. Perhaps one day we are tired and hungry, and then someone cuts in front of us in line at Starbucks. This minor frustration is the final insult that causes an avalanche of emotions to bury us. Journaling allows us to release our pent-up emotions, so we can see each situation independently without being buried in similar feelings from the past.

➡ TRY THIS

You can write about your anger in the form of a letter to the person who hurt or offended you. At the time, your feelings about the situation may have been unconscious or unacceptable. Sadness and worry are often associated with feeling vulnerable, and you may have used anger to protect yourself from those feelings. Writing about what happened now allows you to bring those feelings into your conscious awareness, which is the beginning of healing. Use these focusing questions to start getting beyond the smoke and mirrors of defensiveness and anger:

- *What is the worst part?*

- *How does this circumstance make me feel?*

- *When in the past have I felt this way?*

As you write, you will be making internalized, unconscious, unacceptable feelings conscious and concrete. This allows you to find relief from conflicting logical and emotional reactions, which helps you move forward.

After answering the questions, return to the first one and repeat the process to get to a deeper meaning behind your anger. Continue to repeat this exercise, responding to the questions, until you uncover some seemingly unrelated memory or experience that is still causing pain. The process of uncovering painful memories is like peeling an onion—it may make us cry, but it's how we get to what heals us. Here are some additional focusing questions. Fill in the blanks where necessary to fit your situation:

- *What am I trying to achieve?*

- *How will this affect my life in the long term?*

- *What would be an ideal outcome?*

- *What advice would I give to someone else in this situation?*

- *How come I care so much?*

- *Who was I angry at when that happened?*

- *How would my life be different if...?*

- *What would happen if I were to...?*

- *Who does that remind me of?*

- *What remedy might work?*

- *What has to happen before I can...?*

- *What am I planning on doing about it?*

- *What did I learn from that event?*

- *What would make me happy?*

To get the most out of writing, you can develop some good journaling habits. Set aside a routine time to write, for example, when you first get up in the morning (good for remembering dreams and for planning) or when you go to bed at night (good for reviewing the day). And you can associate writing with a particular place, such as a desk, a comfortable chair by a window, or at a park or coffee shop. You can even use props, such as a favorite pen or a special bound notebook.

10. Meditation

Meditation techniques can reduce anger and increase relaxation. Meditation helps to clear the mind and practice the concept of *letting go*. By learning to let go of thoughts during meditation, we can also develop the ability to let go of sources of frustration in our lives.

A simple meditation technique practiced twenty minutes per day can help you control anger, improve cardiovascular health, and achieve greater capacity for relaxation.[2] Start by practicing regularly, when you are not feeling angry, to make it easier in times of conflict. For many, it is helpful to practice in a seated posture. Lying down may lead to falling asleep, while a seated posture allows for relaxation and muscle balance. Sitting on a yoga mat in a cross-legged posture provides good stability and balance, or you may choose to sit in a chair if you have limited flexibility or motion.

➡ TRY THIS

There are many types of meditation, and there is no one approach for everyone. The meditation exercises that follow can help to calm the mind (through mantra) and body (through movement).

Mantra Meditation

This helps to bring our awareness into the present moment, the here and now. Begin by sitting quietly in a position that is comfortable for you. Select a word or phrase—you can use *in, out* as when doing a breathing technique, or you can use another word like *peace, joy, trust,* or *calm.* Close your eyes or gently gaze on a point in front of you. Relax the muscles and bring your awareness to your breathing. As you breathe in and out, repeat the word or phrase that you have selected.

Let this word go over and over in your mind like an echo

Repeat the word to yourself over and over and over

Simply attend to the word in your mind at your own speed

Repeat it to yourself at your own pace and volume

There is nothing you have to do

No effect you have to achieve

Whenever your attention wanders or you are distracted, simply return to the word and let it echo in your mind.

While practicing this technique, it is helpful to set aside five to ten minutes in the morning to get the day off to a calm start; as the day progresses, it may be more difficult to make time for this activity. You may choose to extend this meditation time as you become more comfortable with this technique.

Movement Meditation

This technique helps us to connect with our body to bring about a sense of peacefulness and relaxation. Begin by sitting quietly in a position that is comfortable for you. Now think of all the times in life you have encountered the gentle movement of rocking:

Perhaps swaying in a hammock or sitting in a rocking chair

Perhaps floating with the tide or bobbing through waves

Or even as a small child rocking in your mother's arms

At this time, let yourself begin to rock back and forth

Let each movement become more and more gentle and easy

Let yourself sway effortlessly

Feel your body rocking on its own, in its own way, at its own speed

Let each movement become more and more subtle

All you have to do is quietly attend to the repetitive back-and-forth movement

And every time your mind wanders or is distracted by thought

Gently return to your subtle rocking motion

For the next minute or so, let your rocking be barely noticeable and quietly attend

When your thoughts wander, simply return to the gentle sway of your body.

Meditation is a way to help you change your relationship to your emotions, in particular strong emotions such as anger. You might not be able to make anger go away, but you can change how you respond or react whenever that emotion arises. The calm that comes from meditation increases patience and reduces reactivity.

11. Progressive Muscle Relaxation

Anger difficulties can make us so tense throughout the day that we don't even recognize what being relaxed feels like. Through practice, however, we can learn to distinguish between the feelings of a tensed muscle and a completely relaxed muscle. By tensing and releasing, we learn not only what relaxation feels like but also how to recognize when we are starting to get tense during the day.

Progressive muscle relaxation (PMR) teaches us how to relax our muscles through a two-step process. First, we systematically tense particular muscle groups, such as our neck and shoulders. Next, we release the tension and notice how our muscles feel when we relax them. This exercise will help us lower our overall tension and stress levels and help us relax when we are feeling angry. To get familiar with PMR, you can start by doing this seated or lying down. Once you feel comfortable with this practice, you can do it more informally whenever you feel the need to relax.

 **TRY THIS**

Begin by focusing on the shoulder muscles (shrugging, pulling them back, pulling them down).

··· SHOULDERS ···

Squeeze the shoulders now

Create a nice good shrug

Hold the tension, nice and tight

Allow the feelings of tightness to grow

And let go

Let your muscles begin to unwind

Feel your body become looser and more limp

As the tension flows out

Let your muscles feel relaxed and soothed

··· ARMS ···

This time, focus on your right arm

Squeeze your lower and upper arm together, bending at the elbow

(Imagine that you are trying to touch your shoulder)

Press tighter and tighter

Let the muscles get nice and hard

Notice the feelings of tension

Hold for count of ten

And let go

Release the tension from your arm

Notice the warm feelings that relaxation brings

Let the tension melt away

Do the same for your left arm

Feel your muscles become more deeply relaxed

· · · FEET · · ·

This time, focus on your right foot

Tense the muscles in your right foot and toes now

(Curl your toes while pushing your leg down toward the floor)

Create a good strong feeling of tension

Let the tension grow

Hold for a count of ten

And let go

Let the tension flow out

Do the same thing with your left foot

As you sink deeper into relaxation

Notice the pleasant feelings you have created

Progressive muscle relaxation is an effective strategy for anger management because it helps us distinguish between the feelings of a tensed muscle and a completely relaxed muscle. This in turn teaches us to cue this relaxed state at the first sign of the muscle tension that accompanies anger. Through physical sensations, PMR helps to build awareness about anger triggers and teaches an association between relaxed muscles and a relaxed mental state.

PART 3

BUILDING FRUSTRATION
TOLERANCE

MANY PEOPLE SAY that the rudeness of others—particularly behind the wheel, on cell phones, and in customer service—is the biggest trigger to their anger. But while we can't control other people, we can manage our own expectations. We can use anger management to counterbalance our insistence on getting what we want, when we want it. In the past, when life moved much slower, we welcomed challenges, learning to make do, adapt, wait, or work for lengthy periods to achieve a goal. Today's expectations of instant gratification have become embedded in modern life. This fuels our anger at inconvenience, disappointment, and delays.

Learning to tolerate frustration contributes to the growth of resilience. Resilient people have the capacity to withstand setbacks, to rise to a challenge, to find new ways of solving problems, and to know that anger-fueled interactions can be managed. Sometimes struggle is exactly what we need in our life. If nature allowed us to go through life without any frustration, we would not be as strong as we are. Tolerating frustration is hard, but that is what gives value to our accomplishment.

This section is about how we take things personally and then deal with the consequences—getting angry or launching into battles over right and wrong. As you grow a thicker skin and learn some skills to tolerate frustration, you can move beyond defensiveness and into a stance of self-control, self-confidence, and greater self-respect.

12. Don't Take It Personally

People who are angry often take things personally and expect criticism from others. If someone doesn't speak to us in a shop, we may think that person dislikes us, when in fact it may be that they are shy or worried about something else. If someone looks over at us, we may think, *He thinks I'm stupid,* when, in fact, the person is just glancing over without any such thought. Sometimes things are just not about you. If someone is cranky and snappy with us, they may be having a bad day and not handling their anger well. It may have nothing to do with us.

When we take others' behavior personally, the assumption is that *Everything is about me.* We may find ourselves feeling miserable because we don't get the approval and recognition we expected. You may say to yourself, *Why does this always happen to me? Or Why does my life have to be so unfair? Or Why is my life so hard?* When we think like this, we secretly imagine ourselves at the center of the universe. This isn't conceit or arrogance; it's called narcissism. It's what happens when we're the point of reference for everything that happens all around us.

When we take things personally, we feel angry and disrespected. Our reaction is either to defend ourselves or shut down but silently stew. Either way, we take someone's criticism and view it as a literal, personal, and serious threat. We want to correct the perpetrators and prove them wrong. We want to maintain our innocence and try with all of our might to defend our beliefs, which only serves to heighten the conflict. In turn, we make something big out of some behavior that is so little.

➡ TRY THIS

We cannot take someone's opinion personally, because the truth is that we are dealing with our own feelings, beliefs, and opinions. No one's judgment is superior; it's only one opinion. It is not about right or wrong; it's just an opinion. Instead of taking things personally, you can catch yourself doing these things and then apply the insights in parenthesis.

- Thinking *This is what you should do.* (*Should* is a preference. Everyone can make their own choices.)

- Demanding others do something our way because we want to get something done quickly. (It's more productive to secure cooperation.)

- Trying to please others. (You don't know how they want to be pleased.)

- Trying not to displease. (Live on your own terms of good enough.)

- Assuming more responsibility then the situation demands. (Allow others to be responsible for themselves.)

- Protecting others from the consequences of their own behavior. (They did not ask for your help.)

- Trying to prevent disaster. (Live in the present; you cannot predict the future.)

- Having perfectionistic standards for others. (You don't really know what's best for them.)

- Trying to prove your worth to others. (Self-worth comes from within.)

By catching ourselves taking things personally, we can choose a different response: self-respect. It then becomes possible to learn from mistakes. If we make a mistake, we are not a screwup. It is not a matter of assigning guilt, fault, and blame. It is a matter of human imperfection: we can make successful efforts and still have undesirable outcomes. We can be a hardworking employee who is punctual and loyal, but we get laid off. We can be a caring and thoughtful partner but still get our heart broken. We can be a careful driver and check our mirrors and put on our turn signal, but someone hits our car. In all these situations, our efforts were commendable, but the outcomes were disappointing. Yet we are worthwhile, regardless.

13. Let Go of Excessive Responsibility

Most adults are responsible. They pay their bills, show up to work, and brush their teeth. Some people go a step further and take ownership over others' happiness. We can be excessively responsible. We feel responsible for fixing others' problems and try to make others understand the error of their ways. When someone is sad, if we take excessive responsibility, we feel it's our obligation to make them happy. If someone is upset, we feel it's our responsibility to calm them down. If two people can't get along, we feel it is our responsibility to help them see the other's point of view. If someone is hurt, we feel it is our responsibility to soothe them. If someone is sick, we feel it's our responsibility to cure them. If someone is having a bad day, we feel it is our responsibility to make it better.

Parents are responsible for the well-being of their children. If they aren't responsible, it's called neglect. However, adults are responsible for themselves. Yet many of us treat other adults like children and seek to control their behavior and decisions. Often, we try and fail. So why do we do it? This self-imposed task of changing others for their own good is based on the presumption that we know what's best. The truth is that we are all imperfect and make mistakes, and striving for perfection sets us up for feelings of failure, yet we may do it anyway. This contradiction causes stress in the form of physiological and emotional discomfort. We feel angry and powerless to do anything about it. In time, we give up on others we care about. We feel disappointed and guilty. You may say to yourself, *Where have I failed?* as if the fault were yours.

➡ TRY THIS

We talk too much, we think too much, we worry too much, we blame too much, we anticipate too much, we calculate too much. The antidote to all of these useless mental gymnastics is to do something in reality and to do it without (or with less) judgment. We can shift our *have-to* thinking to promote a *get-to* mindset, which allows us to see life through a series of choices and feel a sense of opportunity in our actions. It is a mistake to define our self-worth in terms of how much we accomplish and how well we do it. This implies that if we do not perform the task well enough or fast enough, we are worthless, and there is no middle ground.

Being good enough involves taking risks to live up to your own standards of success. If you look for others to tell you when you are good enough, it's like running a race where someone keeps moving the finishing line. A good partner does A, B, and C. Then, after you do it, your spouse says, "A good partner does A, B, C and X, Y, Z." This will leave you feeling frustrated, because no matter how much you do, it is never good enough.

Just do what you can do, and as much as you can do today, that is enough. If you do even more tomorrow, that's all right too, but the beauty of this intervention is that you are a worthwhile human being in the meantime. Here are some ways to set limits around your responsibilities.

Take time for yourself. Develop a belief that everyone needs at least thirty minutes a day to relax, be alone, and sit with yourself.

Become more flexible. Some things are worth not doing perfectly, and some issues are good for compromising on. Is this a hill you really want to climb?

Have an optimistic view of the world. Believe that most people are doing the best they can. Trust people to cope with the consequences of their own choices.

If you can bring yourself to do what you can, you will break out of this prison of anger-inducing absolutes and find the middle ground between impossible, paralyzing extremes of failure and perfection.

14. Accept Yourself

We all want to be better than we are. We want to be smarter, happier, thinner, richer, wittier, more popular, more lovable, or more successful than we are right now. The list goes on. We can't see why we should settle for being less than all we can be. We want to fulfill ourselves, live up to our high potential. We get no points in our own eyes for coming in second. It's absurd.

The requirement that we strive to be better is a problem because we don't know how good is good enough. If we believe that *I must be better than I am*, it's a problem since this belief cannot tell us when to stop bettering ourselves. This belief cannot tell us how much is enough. In the absence of such input, we find ourselves running a race where the finish line keeps moving.

You strive to be better but end up feeling angry from an underlying sense of inferiority, inadequacy, worthlessness, and guilt. This compounds your anger and leads to exaggerated outbursts. To relieve these painful feelings, you resolve to do better next time, still not knowing how good is good enough. We need to stop shifting our standards every time our circumstances change. Our standards are what we use to judge whether something is good enough, clean enough, pretty enough, done well enough.

⟶ TRY THIS

Stop agreeing with your negative thoughts. It's better to just notice them and not give them that much weight. You don't have to take them so seriously. For example, if someone came up to you and said, "You're a purple elephant," you would probably not get insulted. This is because there's no agreement that you have that goes *I believe that I might be a purple elephant, and that is a bad thing.* On the other hand, if someone said to you, "You're cheap," you'd likely get very upset.

If you are upset by that statement, it's because somewhere in your mind you have an agreement that, one, you might be cheap, and two, being cheap is a very bad thing. So when someone points that out, or you see an advertisement for a new car, your mind comes up with *I'm such a loser,* and you agree with it. That hurts.

But you don't have to agree. Not agreeing with negative thoughts is different from arguing with them or resisting them. If someone said, "You're a purple elephant," you probably wouldn't argue about how you really aren't one and how even purple elephants have feelings—you would just shrug and say, "Okay, whatever." You would have no charge on it. That's the attitude to cultivate with your negative feelings and thoughts—a mental shrug. *Okay, that's what my mind is doing, whatever.*

When we stew, chew, or brood, we are investing our energy in an angry thought and, in turn, increasing its significance. By not giving significance to angry thoughts, we rob them of their impact and reduce their ability to reoccur. We achieve this by doing the following:

- Bringing down the significance of our mistakes from unforgivable crimes to mere human imperfections

- Bringing up the level of our self-worth from a contemptible failure to that of an imperfect human being

- Living in the middle ground between the extremes of perfect and worthless by embracing our complexity.

It's not our liabilities or our strengths that define us. We are both.

15. Find Forgiveness

When you increase your tolerance for frustration, you foster forgiveness. If someone hurts you—a friend betrays you, your relative steals from you, your spouse has an affair—you want to lash out in anger. When you can't hit back, your frustration can feel extreme. Why shouldn't you seek revenge? Why should you ever forgive anyone who betrays you? These are legitimate questions. And the answers have to do with an important fact: forgiving bad behavior is not the same thing as forgetting or condoning the behavior.

We may imagine that nursing old wounds puts us in control and prevents the humiliating exposure of our emotions—an exposure that some perceive as weakness. We may even entertain fantasies of someday achieving revenge by hurting the people who have hurt us. Does this dream of vindication in the unspecified future make us happy right now, or does it merely prevent us from living our life? Our anger is pushing us to put these people first and ourselves last. Life is too short for this petty spitefulness. We pay a high price for reserving the right to be as cruel to others as they were to us.

 **TRY THIS**

Forgive others. Your act of forgiveness is for your own benefit, not anyone else's. It's an old truism that holding a grudge against someone is like drinking poison and waiting for the other person to die. When you seek revenge or wish someone else harm, the bitterness of your feelings depletes your energy and prevents your pain from healing. But when you increase your tolerance for frustration—that is, your tolerance for not lashing out when others hurt or disappoint you—you can learn more about the world and discover new opportunities to grow and stay healthy, because you're developing the power to let go of the past and enjoy your life in the present.

We can also choose to replace our old guilt-and-punishment mindset with one that's oriented around regret. *Guilt* means we are wrong and need to be punished. We don't want to feel that way. When people offer evidence, it rarely causes us to change our mind, and it makes us angry. *Regret*, on the other hand, is the wish that things were different from how they are. We recognize that they aren't different. This thing happened, and it's regrettable.

You can say "I'm sorry." Saying "I'm sorry" is not an admission of guilt. Saying "I'm sorry that it happened" is a statement of regret. It's like when someone passes away, and we say "I'm sorry for your loss." We're not taking ownership over the other person's loss, but we regret their pain. Saying "I'm sorry" is a sign of personal strength and self-respect. We are not a criminal worthy of punishment. We can replace our fictitious guilt with the regret that we are not perfect, which only confirms our humanity.

Human mistakes and imperfection are regrettable but forgivable. In the privacy of our own heart, we can identify the anger and choose to forgive the other person: *I forgive you for what you've done, for being so terribly imperfect.* It is not for their good that we are doing this; it is for our own relief. We earned this relief, and we deserve it. We never have to let the other person know about it. We don't have to give them the satisfaction. It's none of their business. This is our choice too!

Here are some choices we can make to foster forgiveness:

1. **Identify the hurt and pain** (what someone just said or did) as antagonism that was meant to provoke us. It was not said or done for us; it serves the other person's agenda.

2. Put our hurt and pain in its proper perspective—the other person's statement or action was immature or childish. It does not deserve the attention and energy we are giving it.

3. Ask if we are going to let our hurt determine our response, or will we choose to use our adult judgment? Are we going to let our anger control us, or are we going to manage it?

4. Identify that this is an opportunity to allow others to be responsible for themselves.

5. Consciously choose to manage our hurt and anger appropriately. We can take in this immature, foolish remark, or we can act like a grown-up instead of returning to our childhood.

6. Let go of our intention to control the situation. We can focus instead on controlling our reactions to the provocation.

We can push our comfort zone by taking the risk of doing something new. We can choose to say, "This is unacceptable.

What are you trying to achieve?" We are not attacking. We are telling the truth. We have the choice to hang on to our pain or to let it go. We can choose to forgive someone, so we can gain the energy back that we've used to hold on to this painful event. It's entirely up to us.

16. Have a Thick Skin

What does it mean to have a thick skin? Elephants and other pachyderms can fend off insects with their thick skins, but we humans can easily get stung not only by insects but by others' words. For us, having a thick skin means not getting bothered or very upset when other people criticize us. It means not taking others' actions personally or as a reflection of our worth.

So how do we not take it personally when someone says, "You're a pain in the ass?" Well, what does it mean when we're a "pain in the ass?" Is it literal? Do you cause a physical pain to occur in their rear? No, it means we are being insulted. We aren't taught how to cope with this stuff in school. Our teacher may have told us to ignore it when someone calls us names. But how did it work out for us? Terribly.

➡ TRY THIS

Separate yourself emotionally from what other people do. Detachment is one of the most valuable techniques available to stop yourself from taking the behavior of others personally.

Detachment occurs when we are able to separate the act from the actors, the people from their behaviors, the sin from the sinners. If someone we love had the flu and cancelled plans with us, we would understand. We wouldn't take it personally or blame them for being inconsiderate or weak. Instead, in our mind, we would probably separate the person from the illness, knowing that it was the illness, rather than our loved one, that caused the change of plans. That is detachment.

But it is important to remember that establishing personal boundaries through emotional detachment is not the same as building walls. Our goal is to heal ourselves and our relationships with other human beings, not to coldly distance ourselves, especially from the people who matter most. If you find yourself consumed with what someone said and dwelling on frustration, try asking yourself the following questions:

Is this really a problem at all? If you view what happened in a different way, is it actually an opportunity to do something well? If you can deal with the situation, then this will be a major triumph for you. If you take the problem on, then you will learn from it, whatever the outcome.

Is this a problem anyone else has or has had? If it is, find out how others have dealt with it, or just talk to them to share the problem; they may be glad to talk. If you are facing a problem at work, talk to older or more experienced colleagues whom you trust. They will probably have seen the problem before and may be able to help you put things in perspective.

Does it really matter anyway? If everything goes wrong, will it really matter anyway? If it does, will it matter in six months or a year? Bear in mind that you will probably have plenty of opportunities to correct any failure or to shine in other ways if things go wrong. As long as you have made your best effort, and learn from any mistakes you make, then you cannot do any better.

How can you focus on the present? If you're holding on to old hurts and resentments, your ability to see the reality of the current situation will be impaired. Rather than looking to the past and assigning blame, focus on what you can do in the here and now.

Do you want to pick this battle? Conflicts can be draining, so it's important to consider whether the issue is really worth your time and energy. Maybe you don't want to surrender a parking space if you have been circling for fifteen minutes, but if there are dozens of spots, is arguing over a single space worth it?

When is it time to let something go? If you can't come to an agreement, agree to disagree. It takes two people to keep an argument going. If a conflict is going nowhere, you can choose to disengage and move on.

Learning to detach means learning to take a moment before reacting to someone else's behavior. At that moment, we can ask ourselves, *Is this feeling about the person or about the situation?* This distinction makes us better able to emotionally distance ourselves from others' actions.

17. Your Power of Choice

Just as we have choices about how to interpret events, we also have options about how to express the anger we experience. Often we limit our range of options by erroneously believing that there are only two choices: either directly expressing anger to someone else (such as in a personal confrontation) or *swallowing* the anger and keeping the feelings to ourselves. In actuality, there are many ways to respond to our feelings and express ourselves.

Suppressing anger is not the same as control. We are merely stuffing it for fear of the consequences of letting it out. Many people may have learned to suppress anger for fear of the consequences of letting it out. Expressing anger as a child was followed by severe punishment from an adult. Stuffing it now is how many of us prevent what we see as disaster (punishment) in the future. The lesson we learned as children became a blueprint for coping with difficult situations in later life.

Too much emphasis on our anger compounds it. If we are angry, and we act on it too much, we are strengthening our anger and making it worse. The same is true with any other emotion. Take fear, for example. If we are scared of something, acting out our fear by screaming and crying every time we come across it simply makes our fear stronger. Too little emphasis on anger, on the other hand, often leads to repression. At best, we become an emotionless zombie: we can't feel anything, for cutting off our "bad" emotions leads to not being able to feel any emotions. We lose touch with an important part of ourselves. The worst-case scenario? It piles up, and we explode.

➡ TRY THIS

Consider the options. We can easily say, "They made me feel..." or "I had no choice but to yell back." This is absurd. We always have choices, but sometimes we just don't like our options. Specifically, we have power over how we interpret others' statements and control over what comes out of our mouths. We can choose to shift mental gears and set limits by doing the following:

- We can choose to respond, not react. We can slow down and keep the significance of the situation in perspective. There is no urgency to act.

- We can choose not to take others' words as fact. We can agree that they feel the way they feel, but we can keep our version of the facts to ourselves. This is called *discretion,* which is the power to choose how much we wish to reveal and when.

- We can choose not to argue or shout when others yell or blame us. We can choose to catch ourselves about to explain, defend, debate, cajole, nag, or antagonize and decide not to do it.

- We can choose to stay calm. We are consciously choosing to give this criticism all the significance it so richly deserves: namely none. Others do not have the power to provoke us. Their words are not for us. There is no need to respond.

We can choose to listen and appear to be paying attention. Nodding our head would be a nice touch. We are not being passive. We are choosing to stay calm and take some deep breaths. We are not taking the bait. Criticism from others cannot be taken as a reflection on our worth. They do not know what's best for us and do not have any standing on which to judge us.

18. Don't Give Advice

The media is full of experts giving people advice. They tell us how to be good parents, loving spouses, supportive friends. The press is full of tips for handling our aging parents, our difficult bosses. The problem is most of the advice doesn't work. Other people may be trying to help us by telling us what to do, but it only perpetuates dependency. It makes us feel like there is something wrong with us for feeling the way we do and being the way we are. This only compounds our anger.

There are many reasons why such superficial, impersonal advice doesn't have deep and permanent effects. In my opinion, it is because these recommendations are based on generalities; a one-size-fits-all, lowest common denominator approach. For specific situations, these experts can't give any answers since they don't know:

1. What the underlying issues are for us

2. What any of us are trying to achieve

3. How we actually feel

4. What our expectations are

5. Our unique context and circumstance

Such advice is preceded by a judgment or an evaluation, which is based on an interpretation of the situation. It prescribes a goal, but it doesn't tell us how to remove the obstacles that keeps us from achieving success. Likewise, when we give unsolicited advice to others, we may sincerely intend to help or assist someone, but our advice sends a variety of underlying messages, which are all based on assumptions and are almost always perceived as negative. When we give unsolicited advice, the implied assumption is:

- "You can't figure this out on your own,"

- "I don't trust you to figure it out."

- "I know and you don't, so I have to tell you."

- "I need to give you the benefit of my advice to validate or to prove to myself how smart I am."

If someone else isn't ready for or doesn't want feedback, it's counterproductive to offer it. The need to give others unsolicited advice is rooted in unexpressed anger. As a result, our advice often comes across as judgmental, authoritative, or self-serving. Our focus is on others rather than where it should be: on ourselves. We need to manage our own anger by expressing it naturally and constructively, so we can stay in our own lane.

➡️ TRY THIS

Stop dishing out advice to others. Much of the advice we think is helpful actually has the opposite effect. It makes the situation worse and causes people to feel angry or misunderstood. If we find ourselves frustrated—because we are trying to help by offering others what we think is really great advice, and they're not taking it—it's time to change tactics. We need to let other people be themselves rather than tell them how to be. Our goal is to refocus and strive to live a life filled with genuine joy, love, and peace.

Specifically, we can catch ourselves wanting to give someone what we are sure is good advice: "This is what I would do" or "This is what we should do." Do not give advice. Instead, you can find out what is preventing someone from taking appropriate action on their own behalf. Here are some additional steps.

- Stop and be silent when feeling the impulse to tell other people about themselves. Practice listening to their feelings, perceptions, and opinions without judgment when the impulse to spout advice arises.

- Before offering an opinion, check within. If your intuition confirms it's all right, lovingly ask if it's okay and receive permission before plunging ahead: "I'd like to give you some feedback. Is that okay?" If you get a no, you can ask a couple more times to see if they want to reconsider—but a consistent no means no. If you get a yes, ask again to make sure the other person is not just being polite.

- If someone is open to what you have to say, you can go forward with kindness, offering an opinion, and without arguing with the other person's reaction or trying to convince.

- Let others know that you can elaborate if they want additional information.

- Accept that we each have our own personal truth.

- Recognize we are only accountable for ourselves. Spend energy on living life with respect and personal integrity.

People give advice for all kinds of reasons, often because we mean well and really want to help. But wanting to help is not the same as actually being able to help. When you find yourself angry on the receiving end of advice from would-be helpers, acknowledge their kind intentions, but feel free to disengage from any obligation to follow their suggestions.

PART 4

MAINTAINING A
POSITIVE OUTLOOK

OUR OUTLOOK TOWARD LIFE, more than any specific events or the people we know, affects how we feel about life. If we see the world as a terrible place, other people as unfair, or life as having the cards stacked against you, we create a formula for anger, sadness, or worry. Say you are leaving for work on a dark, cold, wet morning and you hear the announcer on the radio describe the terrible traffic. You let out a big sigh of anger and feel exhausted before the day has even begun. Then you glance in the rearview mirror and see your child in the backseat, quietly smiling at you, holding his favorite truck. He is delighted with your company and content being in the safe, dry car.

This is how the same event can be perceived in two totally different ways depending on our focus—and you do have a choice about what to emphasize. You have to think like a mechanic who hears a car with a screeching noise. How would you solve the problem? You would begin by trying to identify what conditions triggers the noise: does it happen when the car is accelerating, or shifting gears, or turning at slow speeds? If you can give the screech a context, you can find the broken part. Likewise, it can be helpful to interpret anger-inducing circumstances based on a gradual examination of what's going on. If patterns of negative thinking can be identified and put in a more manageable perspective, we will be less vulnerable to overreacting with anger.

This section explores strategies to change your perspective and reduce anger. This content also looks at the growth and power that comes from focusing on yourself and your own happiness, knowing and asking for what you want, and setting your own standards for self-worth.

19. Increasing Acceptance

Most children play games and learn about taking turns. They learn about sharing and will say it's unfair when someone has a shiny red ball and they do not. Disparity causes pain, and that pain causes hurt, which makes them angry.

As adults, many experience anger from unfairness in their daily lives. Some feel others have all the advantages and privileges. We are socialized to see two groups: the haves and have-nots. This lack of equality is frustrating and leads us to feel disrespected and resentful.

Anger from unfairness may arise if a family member speaks in a sarcastic tone of voice, while you have been polite. It is displayed when a coworker gets promoted ahead of you, when you have put in extra hours. It is experienced when traffic is at a standstill and you have a plane to catch. It's not fair when the bills pile up no matter how much you work; the dog pees on the rug after you have just cleaned the house; when a friend fails to keep a promise after you have lent him money; when a boss criticizes you for something you didn't do; when a child refuses to obey you, no matter how much you praise them; when you are feeling ignored, even though you have given extra attention to others.

Focusing on what is and isn't fair means focusing on the way things should be rather than on the way things actually are. We can all agree that things should be fair, but we won't always agree on what fairness means in a particular situation. If you're struggling with anger, you may tend to believe that fairness means getting your way. And let's face it, we don't always get our way.

→ TRY THIS

When life is not going well, choose to acknowledge what you cannot alter, and look at how to change what you can. Some things we cannot change, but we can choose how we see it, and acceptance is one of those choices. For a person who struggles to control the uncontrollable, acceptance is a change. Learning to accept life as it is and appreciating what we have is essential to managing anger. Here are some tips to find acceptance by focusing on what you can control.

Prioritize. Continually check in with yourself to see that you are working on the most important things that need doing on any specific day. Helping your child talk through a problem they are having or discussing the day's events with a spouse may be more important than getting the dishes done or a load of laundry completed. Don't think of priorities only as jobs that need doing. As you remind yourself to direct yourself to the most important tasks first, you will find yourself letting go of tasks that really did not need doing after all.

Break down large changes into manageable pieces. One source of anger is the feeling of being overwhelmed by what needs to be done. Learn to break down large goals into manageable pieces, and then begin with a piece you know you can handle. The most challenging step on major undertakings is often the first one. Besides, you will have a greater sense of satisfaction as you complete each individual portion of the task and this can keep you motivated to the end. Think of a major task you have ahead of you. How do you get started? What comes next?

Learn to say no. It is not that saying the word is so difficult. It is more the feeling of guilt that some experience as soon as they say it. Try focusing on the important things that will get done because you used that two letter word to decline something which was not a part of your priorities.

Assume ownership of your time. Most people would be surprised if someone reached in their wallet without asking and helped themself to the money found there. But how different is that from letting others help themselves to your time? Take ownership of your own time, and do not allow others to commit your time without your permission. It is not selfish to stop others from squandering your time. Give your time freely when you want, but don't make the mistake of undervaluing this resource or feeling angry when others waste it.

20. Self-Respect

Anger is like fire: it cannot survive without fuel. The fuel that keeps our anger burning can come from many sources, such as problems at work or at home, frustrations with the world, or our inability to overcome the challenges we face. But another big anger source—and one over which we have more control—is self-sabotage; the things we do, perhaps unwittingly, to keep ourselves angry.

You might ask, why would anyone want to be angry? As an emotion, anger can be extremely powerful and seductive, especially if we like to be seen as strong, unflappable, or in control. For those of us who have little joy or pleasure in our lives, the thrill of anger's excitement might be the strongest feeling we have, and even a bad feeling might seem preferable to feeling nothing at all.

We may secretly stoke the fire of our anger. How? One way is to turn our anger against ourselves physically. Perhaps this comes in the guise of something ordinary and culturally accepted, like smoking or drinking; perhaps it's more sinister, like the use of drugs or self-inflicted wounds. Maybe we stop attending to our hygiene or eat our way to obesity. Maybe we stop taking life-saving medications or we drive recklessly. For each of these behaviors, we undoubtedly have justifications, and we rarely recognize that they help to keep us angry. The more we indulge in such actions, the less attractive we are to others, and, simultaneously, the more we blame others for criticizing, mistreating, and misunderstanding us—something that makes us angry!

A pattern of putting ourselves into difficult situations and then blaming others for our failures is another self-sabotage maneuver. Perhaps we begin a relationship based on what we imagine our partner could be, their potential; maybe we accept a job that's inappropriate except in our fantasy of what the job could be; maybe we start a project that's far beyond our skills or budget. In each case, we've set ourselves up for failure and when, in fact, we fail, we angrily blame our partner, our boss, or the world.

➡ TRY THIS

To promote a healthy and happy life, deal with your own anger. You can choose to change your idea that if people behave unfairly toward you, it's a challenge to your worth as a person and they must be confronted. This old pattern only shows that you are trying to control people and that you rely on their approval and acceptance to feel good about yourself.

Managing anger does not lie in controlling the world around you; it arises from self-respect, which is the feeling that you are unconditionally lovable. You are born lovable and worthwhile. You will never be worth more or worth less. You will never be superior or inferior. Once you come to that conclusion, you will be free of the belief that life is threatening and that you must use anger to cope with it. Here are some ways to promote self-respect and let go of anger:

- You can remind yourself that imperfections are simply mistakes and *This does not define me.* You have made many good decisions and have made mistakes before. You are more than the sum of your successes and mistakes. You are complex, not all good or all bad. Your performance will vary from day to day, hour to hour, and you can separate your performance from who you are.

- You can choose to calm yourself down and put your own anger in a moderate, manageable perspective: *Just because they said it doesn't make it literally true. It is how they feel in the present. It's not a fact.*

- You can build on your past successes. Your mind may be quick to notice your mistakes and very slow to validate your successes. Instead, you can consciously choose to remind yourself, *I did that. I got it done and I made it happen.* That is not conceit or smug self-satisfaction. It is confidence. It is validating your efforts to face a difficulty and get through it as best you can.

You can respect yourself regardless of what's going on in your life. That's because self-respect doesn't depend on getting what you want—a promotion at work, the ideal mate, a higher income—or on your ability to be perfect. Respecting yourself means accepting that you are good enough, no matter what anyone else says.

21. Putting Yourself First

To overcome your current anger, it can help to explore your past emotional experiences, which allows you to understand how to make sense out of your struggles. Sometimes you may look around at your life and wonder what you ever did that landed you in this mess. So much of what you achieve results from a lifetime of decisions, large and small. You choose your clothes, job, relationships, and everything in between. Your choices may lead you to the peak of your potential or leave you meandering in the valleys of doubt and guilt. Yet despite their power, most decisions happen so automatically that you barely even realize you're making them.

Automatic emotional processes allow you to respond to familiar situations quickly and efficiently, whereas controlled logical processes produce responses slowly, demanding attention and mental effort. So, if your life is not exactly where you want it to be, maybe you should change the way you make choices.

 **TRY THIS**

Stop spending so much time trying to make others happy or prevent their unhappiness. Doing this requires us to take the risk of choosing to stop doing what is unnecessary, and instead do something constructive by living on our own terms in the present. This may involve stopping what we think we *should* do and making a different choice on our own behalf.

Many people are not used to putting themselves first, but it is entirely appropriate to make ourselves a priority. We are not being selfish to do this. *Selfish* begins and ends with us; we take care of ourselves and let everyone else be damned. This is *self-preservation,* which means, *I take care of me, so I can be there for everyone else.* To be a good husband/wife, father/mother, son/daughter, brother/sister, friend/employee, we have to care for our own needs first. Self-preservation is putting on our air mask first, so we can help those around us.

There are three steps to arriving at the happiness that comes from taking care of our needs: first, we explore what pleases us; second, we choose to do it; third, we choose not to do what displeases us.

What Pleases You?

The first problem many of us face when trying to manage our anger is that we do not know what pleases us. We have been so busy living up to others' standards of good or bad that we have not had the confidence to develop our own standards. I tell my clients to choose to do something that they would have passed up, out of concern for what others might think. You can decide that you have as much right to do it as anyone else. You can catch yourself about to discount it as *scary, pointless,* or *frivolous.* These are obstacles from your past, which prevents you from changing for the better. You can catch yourself about to reject this opportunity, because it might not turn out perfectly. Instead, you can agree that it doesn't have to.

Choose to Do It

Now we come to a second difficulty, because performing this task requires a choice. Many people are not used to making choices, because they do not trust their own judgment or think it is good enough. Many people feel they must depend on the "superior" judgment of others. But if we don't make choices for our own happiness, who will? Making choices on our own behalf is an act of control. This is no longer merely reacting; this is initiating an action. That can be scary for some. Making a choice for ourselves is hard, and that is why doing it counts as a success, regardless of the outcome.

What Doesn't Please You?

A third step is to ask yourself, perhaps for the first time, *What doesn't please me?* Based on the answer, you can then choose to continue or to stop doing whatever you've been doing. For example, if worrying about what other people think pleases you, then you can choose to continue. If it doesn't please you, however, you can choose to stop! Or if bad-mouthing your spouse gives you pleasure, then you can continue. But if it makes you unhappy, you can choose not to do it.

As the process continues, it occurs to many people that the simplest choice is to stop doing what makes them unhappy. For instance, if nagging our partner about leaving their shoes in the hall pleases us, we are free to continue. If it turns out that we hate doing this, we are free to stop. Instead we can choose to say, "It makes me angry when you do that, I would prefer that you pick up after yourself." When we start to please ourselves, we use our adult judgment to make the appropriate choice as to when, where, and how much we need to say.

22. Changing Your Self-Talk

We all have a running inner dialogue of thoughts. Sometimes this inner self-talk is pessimistic, defensive, or vengeful. By attending to our inner self-talk, we will notice critical thoughts intruding. We may notice *distorted thinking*, which involves angry thoughts that flash into our mind and make us feel worse. People tend to have recurring thoughts that arise again and again when angry:

- *He is looking over here at me and thinks I'm stupid.*

- *They always let me down.*

- *She just doesn't care about me, she is so selfish.*

- *[Expletive!] What a piece of [expletive] junk! Now we're going to be [expletive] late!*

- *[Expletive!] What a [expletive] jerk! He knew this was an important [expletive] meeting! So why is he [expletive] late?*

We need to look carefully at our angry thoughts and try to see if we are making errors in the way we interpret situations. It can help to examine long-held beliefs about anger, and challenge those that are unhelpful.

➡ TRY THIS

Pay attention to your thoughts. The way we think has a lot to do with the way we feel, so changing thoughts from a hateful, negative orientation to a calm, positive orientation becomes essential in managing feelings of anger and disrespect. You can begin by spending fifteen minutes every day capturing your thought process on paper. Looking at your thoughts on paper will help you identify when these thoughts are exaggerated and pessimistic.

You can keep a list of your most common negative thought habits along with positive alternatives for each habitual thought. Refer to this list whenever angry thoughts arise, until you can substitute helpful alternatives from memory or immediately make up new thought alternatives to counter negative thoughts. You can remind yourself:

- *It won't always be like this.*

- *I am responsible for my efforts, not the outcomes.*

- *It's about the journey, not the destination.*

- *Right now, I am okay.*

- *I have put up with disappointments all my life. I can tolerate this one too.*

- *Not getting my way is only a disappointment, not the end of the world.*

- *I don't have to have everything I want. The world was not made just for me.*

- *In order to achieve pleasant results, I often have to do unpleasant things.*

- *I cannot predict the future or prevent things from happening. I can take life as it comes.*

- *I'm cooperating to get the job done as best I can under difficult conditions.*

- *I am not out of control. I have the power to choose to live up to my own standards.*

- *I am not unlovable. I feel that way now because of past experiences. I am no more or less lovable than anyone else.*

- *I am not guilty of any crime. I won't let myself be guilt-tripped.*

- *I do not have to defend myself. I can express regret that this happened.*

- *I am not worthless, only imperfect.*

- *I am not perfect, I'm not required to be.*

- *I am a good person going through a hard time.*

- *I will get through this.*

- *I can handle this.*

- *This feeling will pass.*

- *I am a good person whether others appreciate me or not.*

After identifying your angry thoughts, write several positive statements for each negative one. You can focus on what you can do about a specific problem. Replace unfulfilled longing with realistic goals or plans for change. When you can't do anything to change a problematic situation, you can work toward acceptance.

23. Pushing Your Comfort Zone

Do you believe that anger makes you tough? Do you tend to deny and suppress your other feelings? If so, you may live your life prioritizing strength and toughness and tend to see emotions as a sign of weakness and irrationality. You may look strong, but what appears to be strength is actually over-compensation for feelings of inferiority and inadequacy. This leads to a lifelong inability to enjoy close, supportive relationships.

When we lead a life based on toughness, we tend to confuse:

- Cooperation with submission

- Vulnerability with weakness

- Confidence with conceit

- Independence with loneliness

- Freedom with irresponsibility

- Happiness with selfishness

But when we can identify the lessons we have learned about emotions and how they should be handled, we become more capable of changing how we experience and express anger. Here are some problematic lessons we may have learned in childhood:

- Always treat other people's feelings as more important than your own.

- Never do anything that might make someone else unhappy.

- Don't express anger.

- Getting angry gets attention.

- Ignore your feelings—or, better still, don't even have feelings.

- Don't trust others with your feelings. Keep your feelings to yourself.

- Never trust your feelings. Trust only logic.

- Be happy all the time.

- Men don't cry.

Many people do not recall being taught how to cope with their emotions, but such lessons occurred, whether directly or through observation. We do not easily forget the painful lessons from the past. They became our blueprint for coping with anger from out-of-control situations in life. And we have not reassessed our definition of coping for years.

➡ TRY THIS

It takes courage to manage anger in a healthy way. It takes courage and determination to take something on even though it's hard or frustrating. But you can push your comfort zone to make healthy choices and take calculated risks. We all have choices, even if we do not like our options. To do what is hard or to do what is easy, either way the choice is ours, and there will be a consequence. Hard things cause discomfort and can fuel anger, yet there is value from doing what is hard.

We value gold or diamonds because they are precious and hard to get. We value buying a home, having a career, gaining education, or a developing relationship, because these things take effort. It is up to us. We won't experience the benefits of courage until after we have taken the risk of doing what is hard and unfamiliar. We don't feel confident or successful when we do what is easy. We gain confidence by pushing our comfort zone, knowing that it is hard (like making a change) and doing it anyway.

Pushing our comfort zone also means keeping an open mind and being flexible. When you look back on failures or bad luck, you can't even claim with perfect accuracy that your life would be better had the past been something other than what it is. You can only state that your life would be different. Whether it would be better or worse is something you'll never know.

To challenge this way of thinking—that the grass is greener on the other side—you can remind yourself that this idea that you would be happier is just one theory. In fact, you might not have been happier. Ask yourself, *What's another theory?* This question allows you to explore alternative ways of thinking about the present. For example, that dream job we never obtained—a thought which fuels our anger—actually might not have been very fulfilling. What's another theory? Perhaps that job would have required too many hours. That's a second theory, and what's another? It may have caused us to miss the next job opportunity that will come along. And what about that car accident? Could it actually have served as a wake-up call to help us drive more safely and avoid an even more tragic collision that might have occurred a week later? You have no way of stating with certainty that anything would have been better if events had worked out differently, the way you originally wanted. It's only one theory that life would be better if something had happened your way, and you may very well have been worse off.

Yet, some just can't get their minds around the idea that an unrealized outcome may have been harmful and that plan B may be a better plan. Here are some ways you can push your comfort zone by making new choices:

Be tolerant. People have a right to their subjective emotions, and it is never our job to change their emotional experience. This involves putting our own agenda aside and seeking to understand (not agree with) someone else's point of view. By avoiding disrespectful words and actions, we can resolve misunderstandings faster.

Ask for what we want. We do not have to DIY everything in life. We are allowed to ask others for what we want. Asking someone for what we want isn't a sign of weakness or dependency. It's a matter of cooperation.

Keep a realistic perspective. Do not blow the situation out of proportion. Focus on the reality of the moment. When life makes us angry, we can regard it as a problem to be solved. It might be good or bad in the moment, but no one knows what will happen later as a result. We can adapt to life as it unfolds.

24. Shifting Your Perspective

The mind generally uses the makes-sense-to-me rule, where we take a position, look for evidence to support it, and if we find some evidence, enough so that our position "makes sense," we stop thinking. If someone brings up reasons and evidence that question our position, we may be swayed to change our mind, but we usually make no effort to seek out conflicting points of view or change our mind unless those views are presented to us.

This means that we can easily be swayed to distorted thinking in which our thoughts make us feel angrier. When we're angry, we tend to have the same thoughts again and again. It's important to look for recurring patterns like these:

Ignoring the positive. We focus on the negative aspects of a situation and ignore the positive. For example, we are given many compliments, but we fixate instead on a single piece of negative feedback.

Taking things personally. We look for and expect criticism from other people, and when we find it, we feel hurt. But sometimes things just aren't about us. A cranky person who snaps at us may simply be having a bad day and not handling their own anger very well.

Seeking perfection. We expect too much from ourselves and those around us. When others don't meet our high standards, we feel disappointed and hurt, and our hurt quickly turns to anger. When perfectionism reigns, it's often impossible for us to see that others are consistently supportive of us even though they're not flawless.

Seeing situations as unfair. We believe there's an absolute standard when there's not one. But to say that something is fair or unfair is to make a subjective judgment on the basis of what you want, need, or expect from a particular situation.

Making self-fulfilling prophecies. On the basis of a single unpleasant event, we draw pessimistic, cynical, and defeatist conclusions about life as a whole. We see the world through the prism of our negative thoughts and expect the worst. That's often what we get, as a result.

Thinking in all-or-nothing terms. Black-and-white thinking takes us out of the middle ground where most of real life happens. For example, we feel betrayed when a good friend disappoints us—maybe because we were uncomfortable telling them what we wanted and expected in a particular situation—and the next time we see them, we angrily tell them we will never trust them again.

➡ TRY THIS

To short-circuit this process and prevent the chain reaction of angry thoughts from getting out of control, we can remind ourselves that we have many other choices—like these.

- Instead of perceiving a mistake as criminal, we can choose to perceive it as a result of human imperfection. Seen in this perspective, we are not guilty of neglect, irresponsibility, inadequacy, or failure. We make mistakes, and we can learn from them.

- Instead of being angry at ourselves for our faults and limitations, we can choose to forgive ourselves for being so imperfect. We can reflect on our mistakes to see what we can learn from them, so we can improve in the future.

- Instead of taking others' choices personally, we can remind ourselves that everyone makes mistakes and no one is defined by them. If we can respect ourselves and others in spite of everyone's faults and imperfections, we will be less angry.

- Instead of overcompensating by denying or covering up our mistakes, we can remember that no one is perfect. Specifically, we can catch ourselves escaping into denial to relieve our pain: going to the other extreme, defining our worth as a person in terms of perfection, as though we are above sin and fault. We can remind ourselves that perfect people don't exist, that everyone has their own issues, and we will adapt. These messages can be incorporated into our self-talk to crowd the negative echoes from the past.

We can choose to do what reality requires. It does not require us to wallow in either guilt and anger or self-pity and shame. It requires that we change these exaggerated reactions by using good judgment. Judgment is the soul of decision making. It tells us what reality requires us to do and not do. Getting angry about things won't positively change them or prepare us in any way. We can cope with frustrating things in the future, just like anyone else. We don't need to prevent disaster from happening, because our judgment is good enough and we have been able to cope with whatever happens as it occurs.

Reality may require that we make amends, take accountability, express or validate feelings, or listen to pain. We can make a sincere apology for any inconvenience, disappointment, or pain we may have caused. This involves putting our agenda aside and seeking to understand (even if we do not agree with) someone else's point of view.

25. Focusing on the Positive

The human brain is naturally wired to focus on the negative, which can make us feel stressed and angry even when there are a lot of positive things in our lives. We learn immediately from pain—you know, "Once burned, twice shy." Unfortunately, the brain is relatively poor at turning positive experiences into memories.

Our brain has what scientists call a *negativity bias*—commonly described as Velcro for the bad, Teflon for the good. For example, negative information about someone is more memorable than positive information, which is why negative ads dominate politics. I'm not suggesting that we avoid dwelling on negative experiences altogether—that would be impossible. However, we can train our brains to appreciate positive experiences when we do have them, by taking the time to focus on them and install them in the brain.

➡ TRY THIS

Practice positive thinking. You will feel better about working at a job you dislike if you practice thinking *At least it pays the rent, I sure do like my paycheck,* and *I'm going to do the best I can.* If you are depressed or anxious, instead of dwelling on the worst-case scenario, think of the opposite best-case scenario, like winning the lottery or having a perfect marriage. The two outcomes are equally unlikely; it's absurd to try to predict the future accurately. But, at least by imagining the best-case scenario, you can stop accepting whatever pops into your mind and believing it to be true.

Pick an area in which you are having trouble, then create or invent new memorable, extremely favorable, ridiculously absurd options to deal with that situation. If you are uncomfortable around your supervisor at work or around your relatives, imagine positive scenes in which you solve conflicts or make adjustments. If confidence and self-esteem are low, imagine scenes in which your confidence is higher. Imagine being praised for your efforts, being successful, or finally receiving the acceptance or affection you've wanted from those who have not provided it in the past.

It may not be so simple. For example, say you are fighting low self-esteem because of a negative experience in the past. To change your self-image, you can repeat the affirmation, *I am good, beautiful, worthy, and strong.* However, your unconscious mind sabotages efforts to create a new positive identity by releasing the negative counter-thought, *You are an insecure, awkward, unlovable loser.* This negative thought has had control of your self-image for years. It is a well-established thought circuit that does not give up its power so easily.

The negative thought maintains its power unless neutralized by an even stronger, positive thought. With practice, eventually the positive thought will grow and associate with other positive thoughts such as *I am a good person. There are many successes in my life. People actually do like me. I have a lot to offer.* We can choose at any time to deploy an army of positive thoughts that will rapidly and effectively neutralize the negative ones. Then, when the same provocative situation arises to test us, our mind can remain positive, poised, and peaceful. We can choose to replace our need for outward approval with some self-validation:

- *I am a caring person.*

- *I will deal with it.*

- *I will get through this.*

- *I can do it.*

- *I am a good person.*

- *I am okay right now.*

- *I can handle this.*

There is no danger that these personalized encouragements will go to your head. You will not become smug or arrogant. Rather, you will feel encouraged. It may sound strange, but your brain will think your life is better (it only knows what it's told!), and your mood will gradually lift.

PART 5

EXPRESSING YOURSELF

COMMUNICATION IS 10 PERCENT INFORMATION AND 90 PERCENT EMOTION. Good communication is more than just sending a message. It's like a game of catch: making sure that the message we send is the message received and that the message we receive is the message that was sent. Easier said than done. Effective communication occurs when our actions and words match. If they don't, then the sender or receiver is responsible for offering clarity or asking for it. This requires an awareness of our feelings and how we communicate through words and body language to others.

The wrong kind of talking can be more destructive than no talking at all. Positive communication is informed, relevant, and beneficial. Negative communication is defensive, discouraging, and unproductive. People often say the same things over and over because they don't feel their emotions have been heard.

It's easy for a listener to jump over feelings and give advice, share facts, or try to minimize the problem rather than really hear what's being said. When we refuse to hear someone else's feelings, we are essentially telling that person, "Your feelings are not okay. You have no right to feel that way."

This section explores communication strategies to manage conflict and reduce your anger. This material also offers tools to respond with empathy to others' anger. These strategies can assist with advocating for your own happiness, creating cooperation, seeking compromise, and maintaining your own standards.

26. Do Not Defend

When we are defensive, it is usually an attempt to justify what we did and correct what we feel is a misperception. When we verbally attack others, they may escalate by defending themselves and going on the counterattack. Because discussions like these are about a topic completely unrelated to our honest emotional need, they cannot lead to a solution. The arguments seem empty and endless because they are missing the point. If we are not heard, we cannot communicate our needs. It is understandable, then, that we feel frustrated or worse when we are cut off with a "That's ridiculous!"

We need to avoid explaining why we did what we did, because our defensiveness can make others feel frustrated, unheard, and confused. When we are being defensive, we are focusing all our attention and energy on ourselves as opposed to offering support and understanding to others. The way that we each perceive an event is all that really matters. We need to accept that we see things differently and accept others' perceptions as their opinions. Usually, people just want the opportunity to express themselves and feel that they have really been understood.

This means that validating feelings is important. Rather than doing this, however, we often reply by passively invalidating unpleasant feelings. We may offer a solution to fix a problem, when that's not what the other person is looking for, or offer a platitude like "It's all good. Just chill out." We may not say anything directly that is critical or accusatory, but we may paper over it. We may change the subject: "How about a cup of coffee?" Or we may ignore the emotion altogether and sit in silence, hoping that it will go away. But it doesn't go away. We have only added to the other person's anger.

➡ TRY THIS

Realize that as soon as you defend yourself, you lose. When you respond to someone's criticism, you are making their accusations real, as if they were worthy of rebuttal. But your imperfections are not crimes; you are not a guilty criminal worthy of punishment. The other person is not the judge and jury. Instead, if you can sit with someone's emotional reaction—be curious about it, maybe ask questions and listen for the feelings behind the words rather than rush to explain or defend yourself—you will have a much better chance of addressing the wounds. You can offer the following remarks when faced with someone's anger.

1. **"You must be very angry."**

   The other person may say, "I am not angry." This is called *denial.* They may have learned that it is acceptable to be "upset" but never angry. We are not put off by this defense. We bounce right back, still on our terms. We do not debate over the truth or falsity of these nonrational retorts. Instead, we can agree with "I hope you aren't, because anger is a very painful emotion. But if you want to talk about it, I'll listen." We are standing our ground, letting them know that we do not intend to force our emotional first aid upon them. We are not deceived or distracted by their denial. The issue here is not the name of their emotion. The issue is not truth. We do not say, "Yes, you are angry! Admit it!" The issue is that we are prepared to cooperate and they are not. We can always listen to seek understanding even if we disagree.

2. **"You sound very angry. Did anything happen to make you angry?" Or, "What happened to make you so angry?"**

   This intervention has the advantage of skipping the issue of emotions and focusing on the precipitating factors that caused it. It offers an invitation to get relief by verbalizing the event in a non-threatening, nonjudgmental context. It's not about who is right or wrong. We are offering the other person the opportunity to express their painful anger so the wound can heal properly.

3. **"That must have made you very angry. I'd be angry if that happened to me."**

   By using the word *anger*, we are giving the person's out-of-control emotion a handle they can grasp onto. We are also giving them permission to express the emotion that they are experiencing.

4. **If they say, "I'm so mad, I could scream!" We can choose to say, "I get it. I don't blame you. I feel that way sometimes myself."**

   This technique is called self-disclosure, and it is often the last thing we think of doing, but it can be very helpful. We are not glad that they are angry. We are not glad that they are being unpleasant. But we are glad that they're behaving appropriately under these difficult circumstances to rid their system of this emotional pain. We are validating them as a person in spite of their hurtful behavior. We are bringing this unmanageable anger down to more manageable proportions.

5. **"I'm sorry you are so angry."**

Many people find it hard to say "I'm sorry" when someone is angry. We have learned that "I'm sorry" is tantamount to an admission of guilt: *Why should I say that? I didn't make them angry.* But this expression is really an expression of regret. Regret is the sincere wish that things were not the way they are. We know that anger hurts, and we regret that the other person is in so much pain. When a self-respecting person says, "I'm sorry," with the right tone, it is not perceived as an admission of guilt but as a sincere, heartfelt expression of empathy in a difficult time.

It is hard to listen to anger without going down the path of defensiveness. We can silently remind ourselves that these comments are merely a child's temper tantrum; they don't help the situation. Even if they are true, they are only describing imperfections. They are regrettable, and we wish we didn't make mistakes. But this doesn't make us a bad person. We are choosing to keep our opinions to ourselves for now. They would not listen to what we have to say right now anyway.

27. Dealing with Difficult People

What makes people difficult? Often it's because they have a high need for human intimacy but fear closeness. The need for intimacy brings them toward others emotionally, but their fear of closeness pushes them away. When they become difficult, they are rejected, and their self-fulfilling prophecy of being abandoned is realized. Dealing with difficult people means dealing with difficult behavior. If our response to their behavior is negative, we will contribute to their difficult behavior.

We may not be able to change the behavior—people only change when they want to change—but we can manage our own response or reactions. Knowing how to communicate effectively can influence others in a positive way when we are acting as a model for proper behavior in a difficult situation. Here are the two most common reactions when dealing with difficult people.

We defend ourselves. When someone is rude and angry, we feel attacked verbally. We become defensive and find reasons to excuse the problem. This is an automatic response, but they do not care whether we or somebody else made the mistake.

They just want for the problem to be resolved. This is a no-win situation for us. We become defensive and frustrated. They remain difficult, as the problem has not been solved.

We are upset, but we don't say anything and concentrate on solving the problem. Even though we are not showing our emotions, we are upset and, without realizing it, we are absorbing the other person's anger. Eventually, we will release our anger. We may become irritable with others, like our peer, our supervisor, our spouse, our dog; or worse, we may start drinking to get into a better mood or to relax. This is a no-win situation for us. We are still upset and displace our anger toward others even though they had nothing to do with the situation.

➡ TRY THIS

Dealing with difficult people means having difficult conversations. When having difficult conversations, we should set a time to discuss our concerns. The time must be agreed upon by both parties and must be a priority apart from any unforeseen events. To begin, I suggest inviting the person to talk by scheduling a conversation rather than pushing them into a discussion.

Invitations support cooperation, rather than bullying others into speaking when it's convenient only for us. It can help to ask:

- "Is this a good time to talk?"

- "I want to talk, can we sit down tomorrow after dinner?"

- "I need your help with what just happened. Do you have a few minutes to talk?"

- "I'd like to talk about [name the incident]. When is a good time for you?"

When discussing difficult issues, I recommend turning off music, TV, computers, and cell phones, to remove any distractions to emphasize that this conversation is a priority. Go into the conversation prepared to listen to and consider the other person's point of view. We can show that we are listening by nodding, saying "I see," and rephrasing the other person's key points ("So what you're saying is..."). The purpose of repeating what the other person has said in our own words is not to parrot the other person but to create communication and dialogue and to give ourselves a way to remember what the two of us just talked about.

Then, come right to the point and use an *I-message*. For example, "I felt hurt when..." or "I'm concerned about..." or "I'm feeling really [fill in the blank with an emotion like *sad, scared, frustrated, overwhelmed,* or *stressed*], and I need your help." Third, make a request for what you would like to see happen going forward, such as: "I'd prefer..." And then name something specific and doable, such as "that you text me when you are leaving work."

Be sure to state the request in positive terms. If we say, "Stop doing so and so," we are focusing on the negative and not offering a clear alternative. Confused, the other person may simply continue acting the same way as before. If we want someone to stop shouting, we can, for example suggest, "I'd prefer you talk in a calm voice." The idea is that we need to let others know what we want from them.

28. Increasing Empathy

Many statements that we think show understanding actually have the opposite effect. They make others feel dismissed or misunderstood. If their comments are continually passed off as being of little consequence, they will begin to feel that their opinions are not important. Below are some examples of things that we should avoid in our relationships:

Looking for inconsistencies in the story line. This will make our conversation partner feel as though they need to edit their words before speaking, and doing so will impact their ability to authentically express themself. This also creates a dynamic where the facts are given far more importance than they deserve. The emotional expression is more important.

Responding with explanations as to why they are wrong (and we are right). Do not try to argue others out of their emotional experience. Being an empathetic listener allows the other person to heal by giving space for an emotion to be expressed and understood. Being right is irrelevant. Others feel the way they feel. It is irrational and unhelpful to suggest that they should feel or perceive something differently. To do so implies that perceptions and emotions are objective and consistent, which is not true.

Offering an alternative way to perceive the situation. Do not offer forced or contrived optimism. This belittles others' subjective experience and is generally both annoying and aggravating. Giving others the ability to vent their experience and fostering acceptance are the goals. We can help them by listening and reflecting their experience. People want the safety of a nonjudgmental ear. Authentic encouragement is different from forced optimism. Gently saying that we are there for them, or that we will support them, is perfectly fine.

Using tangents to change the subject. Allow the focus to stay on the other person. Bringing up other issues will confuse the interaction and will distract our conversation partner from getting their needs met. As the listener, our job is to listen. At some other time, we can have the space to be the speaker.

Being belittling, sarcastic, or mean. Even as adults, we may find ourselves engaging in these rather immature behaviors. Being mean is a poor way of saying, "I am overwhelmed by what you are saying and feel the need to attack you to get you to stop." Asking for space is perfectly appropriate if we need a bit of time to be fully available for the other person. Never use verbal aggression to attempt to steal power from the speaker.

Making threats or holding the relationship hostage with ultimatums. These manipulative behaviors antagonize the other person's fear of rejection, abandonment, and loss. The attempt to scare someone into agreement leads to resentment, as they feel controlled by our demands for submission. Accusations or criticism will automatically put our partner on the defensive, and instead of finding resolution, we will end up fighting about the last ten things that pissed each of us off.

⟹ TRY THIS

In difficult times, often we really want someone to just be there for us and to show compassion and understanding for what we are dealing with as opposed to offering pragmatic solutions or taking initiative to fix it. In short, people very often simply want empathy and they can feel worse, alone, or misunderstood if the would-be listener goes into problem-solving mode. I would hypothesize that we are conditioned or taught to use our problem-solving abilities with greater frequency or instead of our empathic abilities. It appears that society rewards problem solvers and people that offer tangible fixes with greater effort than it rewards those who offer emotional support. This system of rewards conditions people (especially men) to engage in fixing behaviors rather than empathic behaviors. We know we are being empathic when we can relay the following back to our discussion partners.

- What was their perception of what happened?

- What was troubling to them?

- What were the emotions that they felt at the time?

- What emotions are being expressed at this moment?

- What do they need from us?

The answer to this last question is that they usually just need our empathy. When we are listening to others, it helps to attend to how they felt at the time and how they feel right now as they are retelling the story. They want our support and need us to be emotionally open, so they can safely share their emotional experience. It is rarely important that we understand the specifics of the plot, though we can certainly pay some attention to the details as well. We are helping by just listening, bearing witness to their emotional pain.

29. Agree with It

I often hear clients say, "They made me feel..." or "I had no choice but to yell back." It's one thing to ignore a dumb remark. It's quite another to feel like a doormat, enduring verbal abuse and ignoring the painful degradation of our worth as a person. However, it's not personal when we consider that the other person merely wants to intimidate us and is using provocative words or a hostile tone to show dominance. This is done to push us into submitting.

We can catch ourselves about to take a barrage of insults personally, as if the insults were a reflection on our worth as a person. That is exactly the way the other person wants us to take it! They are building themself up by tearing us down! This tells us that they are in pain. We can choose to not give others verbal ammunition and not tear them down more than they are already.

➡ TRY THIS

We can choose to agree with the feelings, not the facts—agree that others feel the way they feel. We can say, "It's awful, isn't it?" Or, "I don't blame you for being angry." We are not agreeing that they are right. We are just letting them know we heard what they said. We can even say, "It certainly seems like I'm hard to get along with." We are not agreeing with the facts of the matter; we're agreeing that they feel the way they feel.

Feelings are like opinions and perceptions in that they are subjective, without factual basis. When we agree with feelings, we're only saying that people feel the way they feel at the time. We can't talk them out of their nonrational feelings. It is a mistake to try. Why is a spider scary? Some scream and recoil; others grab a tissue and go squish. I don't have to agree that a spider is scary to understand how painful fear is.

By agreeing with feelings, not the facts, you're doing the unexpected. We can agree that it's painful and that this pain hurts, or we can choose to agree that the other person is upset: "It's so frustrating when this happens, isn't it?" We do not need to go on and on, defending the inaccuracy of others' accusations, trying to win a pardon for an unproven offense. We are not required to defend against fiction; they are not a judge and we are not guilty. We do not need to explain our choice to live in the real world. It's not a crime; we do not have to convince them of our innocence. Instead, we can respond to their put-downs by doing something else, such as saying this:

- "I get it."

- "I never thought of it like that."

- "I would be concerned too if I thought…"

- "That's awful."

- "That must be painful."

- "I don't blame you for feeling that way."

- "Thanks for calling that to my attention."

- "I hear what you're saying. I appreciate it, and I'll be fine."

- "That would be nice, wouldn't it? But I'd rather not."

- "I know you mean well and want the best for me, but I prefer to do it this way."

- "I totally agree. I'm just not sure it would help."

- "You may have a point."

- "It seems that way sometimes, doesn't it?"

This is not pleasing or kowtowing or giving others satisfaction. It is taking the wind out of their sails. We are establishing healthy boundaries by depriving them of a target. We are not being mean or angry. We are merely acknowledging that we heard that they said something.

30. Use Tone and Body Language

Why do we raise our voice and begin to yell at people when we argue? Do we tend to raise our voice so we can be the dominant speaker? If so, we may be damaging our ability to be a better communicator and secure cooperation. We all telegraph our needs and feelings, whether we are aware of it or not. Probably over half of the meaning that others attach to our spoken message comes not from the words themselves but from our tone of voice. We may yell when we hit our thumb with a hammer, when we are frightened, or when we are excited, but more often yelling is a sign of aggression.

The feeling conveyed in our voice makes more impact and is remembered longer than the words actually spoken. That's why we can't always recall the exact words someone said but clearly remember how we felt when they said it. The tone (its pitch, volume, and clarity) all combine to give the listener clues about how to interpret the message, conveying the speaker's mood and the meaning behind the words. Yelling or raising our voice can be an attempt to control the situation. We get loud to force the other person to listen to what we have to say and, in turn, comply with what we want or reap the consequences.

However, the person who is saying nothing is rarely listening in this situation. More often, they are waiting for the speaker to pause, so they can lash out with a rebuttal to defend against this verbal attack.

Body language can be as important as tone of voice. If somebody comes closer to us than we are used to, invading our personal space, they can give us an uneasy feeling. We feel inclined to take a step backward. Likewise, if we stand too close, we will be marked as "pushy" or "in your face." Stand or sit too far away, and we will be "keeping your distance" or labeled as "standoffish." So in a group situation, it helps to observe how close the other people are to each other and then adapt how we stand, accordingly. Also, we can notice if we move closer to someone and they back away, we are probably just a tiny bit too much in their personal space, their comfort zone. We've over-stepped the mark and should pull back a little.

➡ TRY THIS

Pay attention to nonverbal signals. The most important information exchanged during arguments is often communicated without words. Nonverbal communication includes eye contact, facial expression, tone of voice, posture, touch, and gestures.

When we're in the middle of a conflict, paying close attention to the other person's nonverbal signals may help us figure out what the other person is really saying, respond in a way that builds trust, and get to the root of the problem.

When someone talks, make an effort to really listen. Stop whatever you are doing, and pay close attention to their tone and words. Quite often what is said between the lines is just as important as the words being spoken. Also, pay attention to nonverbal language and maintain good eye contact. This will ensure that you stay present with the conversation, and a plethora of information is transmitted through someone's eyes. The emotional experience of the speaker is far easier to deduce when we are focusing on their body language. Focusing on non-verbals dramatically reduces misunderstanding and helps us as listeners avoid projecting our own emotional experience onto the speaker's story. Quite simply, we can see how others feel.

Expressing confusion will foster understanding. You know that feeling when you've been on a road trip and have gotten a little lost? You don't know exactly where you are and feel a bit unsure about what to do next. Do you stop and get directions? Do you turn around? Do you pull over for the night? Do you keep going? You are a little concerned and unsure about which path to take. Curiously, communicating that feeling in your tone of voice can be helpful when you're listening to someone who's angry. Really we don't know what's going on and why the other person is making these false accusations. We can speak slow and softer, but deliberate and clear.

Good communicators do not take tone personally. They choose to ask questions to gain understanding rather than give explanations to force agreement. They choose to make the covert feelings overt by responding to the emotions behind words. So it's helpful to make the implied explicit by commenting on what you observe:

- "You sound angry. You're shouting."

- "You look sad. You're crying."

- "You seem worried. You're trembling."

Conflict triggers strong emotions and can lead to life-changing regrets. When handled in an unhealthy manner, it can cause irreparable rifts, resentments, and breakups. But when conflict is resolved in a healthy way, it increases our understanding of one another, builds trust, and strengthens our relationship bonds.

31. Expressing Preferences

Let's imagine someone says, "You never listen to me" or "You always blame me." Taken literally, these *always* and *never* statements are probably not an accurate reflection of the facts. Often we choose to defend against these false accusations. So we offer evidence: "What do you mean I never listen? You asked me to call the plumber, and I did. Here, look at the phone bill. I'll show you." We call our expert witnesses to the stand: "I don't always blame you. Ask my brother. He'll tell you." However, this rarely causes the other person to change their mind and our pleas are disregarded. Thus, we feel like we failed to make our case, which only compounds the guilt and escalates the miscommunication as we retaliate with our own blaming accusations.

Think about how the words *should* and *must* are used in language. These small, single-syllable words limit options and creative problem-solving by fostering rigidity. If we should or must do something one way, then it rules out all the other ways a thing might be accomplished. This fosters a rigid perspective on how we and others are supposed to behave. Rigidity inevitably creates tension between our ideals and the way things really are. *Shoulds* also imply guilt, and guilt is painful. A *should* or a *must* sets up the speaker as a superior authority: "You must do it this way" implies "I know what is right, and you don't." These words change a disagreement between equals into one about dominance and submission, and the question becomes, "Who's right and who's wrong? Who is in a position of superiority and power?"

For example, our parents say, "You should have done it this way." The word *should* implies that they know what is best, and if we don't do as they would have done, then we are guilty of being wrong and need to be punished. We then find ourselves in the imaginary court of law, offering reasons, facts, and defenses for why we shouldn't do as others feel we should. This never works. We end up defending ourselves against someone's false accusations. Our mistake is to take these accusations literally, personally, and seriously. When we do, we make the mistake of choosing to plead our case in an imaginary court of law with a judge and jury of one. Again, we make the mistake of defending our innocence to avoid being convicted as guilty and deserving of punishment.

➡ TRY THIS

We all know there are exceptions to always and never statements and that they are not literal facts. So we need to clarify our language to convey that *always* and *never* are figurative or feeling words. The idea is that "It feels like you never listen to me" or "It feels like you always blame me." By adding "feels like" we avoid sidetracking into debates about whether this does in fact always or never occur. This ensures we are being clear and more likely to be heard and understood.

Likewise, if we express our preference, rather than insist that something should or must be a certain way, we greatly reduce the intensity of our remarks. A *preference* is an individual, subjective response of liking or disliking one thing more than another. A preference usually describes a situation in which not much is at stake. "I prefer this food over that food," but it doesn't really matter too much if I don't get my preference. A preference implies a choice, not a demand. We're offering an opinion of the moment rather than a judgment about the nature of life. A preference implies that our view on right and wrong is relative to our experiences.

We can't argue about taste. Is red a better color then blue? Is steak better than chicken? These are preferences. No one knows what is best for other people or has the absolute authority to tell us how things should or ought to be. Everyone's perception of reality is their own truth. There is no agreed-upon right or wrong, good or bad. We only have personal preferences and individual taste.

32. Effective Communication

Learning to verbalize our emotions simply and effectively might make us feel vulnerable, but it's one of the most important steps we can take to decrease our anger. Here are some ineffective forms of communication followed by examples of how to communicate more effectively in these situations:

Defending our innocence: "But I didn't do it honey, I swear to God." This response is perceived as fighting, as if we are calling someone a liar and accusing them of doing or saying something they never did. The pleas to defend our innocence do not usually have the desired effect of convincing others that their accusation is false. However, our innocence is not the issue here; we are not guilty of a crime and we do not require any defense. Instead, we can simply say, "I would be upset too if I thought that."

Giving orders: "Get a hold of yourself. Back off. Leave me alone." Most people do not take orders, and we cannot make them do anything. Our effort to tell them what we want is useless. A better option is to control ourselves. Our hands are full enough with just ourselves. If we do not look after ourselves, who will? Instead of giving an order, it helps to set limits and say, "I'd like to hear more when you're calm."

Excessive responsibility: "Let me do it. You are screwing it up." When we see others making mistakes and behaving irresponsibly, we may try to assume responsibility for them. We try to take over, which others perceive as an attack. Our accusations push them away. Instead, we can choose to assume appropriate responsibility for our own physical and emotional well-being. We can say, "I can lend a hand if you'd like."

Predicting the future: "I know what you're thinking. Here we go again." When our life in the present is being controlled by someone else, we try to solve this painful problem by escaping into the future. We come up with imaginary solutions, such as "If you don't stop now, there's going to be trouble," "I'll leave you," or "I'll call the cops." These exclamations are accurately perceived as threats, bluffs, and overcompensating for our own feelings of inadequacy. No one is impressed. The other person's hurt becomes even more painful. It is better to stay in the present: "If you want to talk, I will listen."

Appealing to logic: "This does not make any sense. You are acting crazy. You're being too sensitive." We make the mistake of trying to solve emotional problems logically: "Be reasonable, use your head." Our naive attempt to appeal to reason through the use of logical thought is delusional. It assumes that people are like Mr. Spock, all logic, and that with enough information, they will be swayed. We spend time giving evidence and explaining our point, but to no avail. We cannot change their feelings by imposing our logic, because it doesn't compute. It is more effective to validate the feelings behind the other person's words: "You sound really upset."

Forcing agreement: "You are wrong. That's totally false." We make the mistake of trying to persuade the other person to "see reason," to agree with our perception of the reality of the situation. We call them out about the error of their ways. They hear our attempt to make them agree with us as (1) trying to control them with manipulative, irrelevant logic, (2) trying to put them in the wrong when they believe they are right, (3) trying to force them to submit, or (4) trying to make them feel or look stupid. It is more effective to seek understanding by asking them questions like "Help me understand, what angered you the most?"

Denying their anger: "You have no right to be angry at me after all I've done for you." Anger is not a right guaranteed under the Constitution. It is an emotion. When we deny the legitimacy of someone's anger, we are, by extension, attacking them. They take it personally. Now they are really hurt. The exaggerated anger in "You are late" may seem unjustified to us, yet we must remember that these surface issues often conceal a bellyful of unresolved anger from the past. It is no use to argue about the seriousness of the precipitating factor. We can acknowledge the feeling, without agreeing that we caused it: "I don't blame you for being angry. I'd be angry too if I thought that."

Using humor: "Gee, you look kind of funny when your face gets all red like that." This response does not turneth away wrath. This is ridicule, and it suggests that we are not taking the other person seriously. Anger is painful and their hurt needs to be respected. We will not extinguish the fire of anger by pouring kerosene on it. There are times when it is appropriate to lighten up. This is not one of them. Sometimes it is best to simply comment on what we observe: "You sound angry. You're yelling."

 **TRY THIS**

It can be helpful to translate complaints and criticisms into requests. Criticism and complaints put people on the defensive and, as a result, their capacity to listen goes down. It is more effective to translate and restate complaints into requests for action. This is done by asking conciliatory, compassionate questions, which will allow us to move forward, rather than focusing on blame. In addition, we will get more cooperation by using specific, action-oriented, positive language when responding to another's complaints. Here are examples of questions you can ask. Fill in the blanks with your own words as needed.

- "What kind of information do you need?"

- "How can I modify...to solve the problem?"

- "What do you think about...?"

- "It would help me to...if you would..."

- "Will you please...so that...?"

- "In order to...I ask that you..."

When there is confusion, people often ask why someone made the choices they did, as if more information would cause us to suddenly agree with their choices. The mistake here is that questioning why someone did something encourages the speaker to defend and justify why they think and feel what they do. In addition, peppering the other person with questions about why they did something can cause them to get angry. It's no different than a child who asks, "Why is the sky blue?" and we answer "Because of the ocean." And the child asks, "Why is the ocean blue?" and we answer, "Because of algae." This continues, "Why is there algae?" "Because of plankton." "Why is there plankton?" "Just because!" Eventually the cycle of having to defend each answer leads to anger, because the answer is never good enough to satisfy the questioner. Instead of asking why, it helps to ask *what* or *how* questions like:

- "How did it happen?"

- "What was going through your mind when...?"

- "How do you make sense of it?"

- "What are you trying to achieve?"

Managing and resolving conflict involves learning how to listen. When people are upset, the words they use rarely convey the issues and needs at the heart of the problem. When we listen for what is felt as well as said, we connect more deeply to our own needs and emotions and to those of other people. Here are some tips for being a better listener:

- Listen to the reasons the other person gives for being upset.

- Make sure to understand what the other person is telling you—from their point of view.

- Repeat the other person's words, and ask if you have understood correctly.

- Ask if anything remains unspoken, giving the person time to think before answering.

- Resist the temptation to interject your own point of view until the other person has said everything they want to say and feels that you have listened to and understood their message. When listening to the other person's point of view, these responses are often helpful: "I want to understand what has upset you" and "I want to know what you are really hoping for."

- Clarify the real issues, rather than making assumptions. Ask questions that allow you to gain this information and which let the other person know you are trying to understand. "Can you say more about that?" and "Is that the way it usually happens?" are some examples.

- Restate what you have heard, so you and the person speaking are both able to see what has been understood, and to show that you are open to hearing more: "It sounds like you weren't expecting that to happen." "That has to be exhausting. Then what did you do?"

- Reflect feelings and be as clear as possible: "I can't imagine how upsetting that must have been." "That must have been disappointing."

- Validate the concerns of the other person, even if a solution is elusive at this time. Expressing appreciation can be a very powerful message if it is conveyed with integrity and respect: "I really appreciate that we are talking about this issue." "I am glad we are trying to figure this out."

Healthy communication does not have to end in agreement. One of the benefits of regular conversation is the discovery that it's okay, and even stimulating, to disagree. When you have opinions and boundaries, healthy opposition is entirely appropriate and better than rote agreement with everything the other person says. But open-mindedness is essential. You must be willing to listen—and hear—opposing views.

CONCLUSION

ANGER IS LIKE FIRE: it cannot survive without fuel. Like fire, unchecked anger can grow out of control and cause enormous damage and pain. But also like fire, anger can be recognized, controlled, and managed in our lives. The fuel that keeps anger burning can come from many sources—from problems at work or at home, from frustrations with the world, from our inability to overcome the challenges we face. The techniques to extinguish the flames are based on you taking control over your mind and body.

Learning to control your anger is a skill. When learning a new skill, it is important to remember that you will not be an expert straight away and that practice is required for the new skill to become an automatic behavior. With this in mind, it is important to remember not to give up if it doesn't work as well as you would have liked in the early stages.

If you can accept the idea that anger exists for a reason, then you can find the value in every frustration. Finding this value will allow you to understand your anger and express it in more adaptive ways. Remember, you cannot eliminate anger. Life will always be filled with frustration, pain, loss, and the unpredictable actions of others. You cannot change that. But you can change the way you let such events affect you.

NOTES

1 Zlatan Krizan and Garrett Hisler, "Sleepy Anger: Restricted Sleep Amplifies Angry Feelings," *Journal of Experimental Psychology: General* 148, no. 7 (2019): 1239–50.

2 Alexander B. Fennell, Erik M. Benau, and Ruth Ann Atchley, "A Single Session of Meditation Reduces of Physiological Indices of Anger in Both Experienced and Novice Meditators," *Conscious Cognition* 40 (2016): 54–66.

Aaron Karmin, LCPC, is a licensed clinical professional counselor who earned his master's degree through Roosevelt University in Chicago, IL. In addition, Karmin is a certified clinical hypnotherapist, and holds an advanced certification in stress management. He is author of *The Anger Management Workbook for Men*, and his approach focuses on identifying physical cues, recognizing thoughts, considering consequences, implementing solutions, choosing behaviors, and promoting expression.

Real change *is* possible

For more than forty-five years, New Harbinger has published proven-effective self-help books and pioneering workbooks to help readers of all ages and backgrounds improve mental health and well-being, and achieve lasting personal growth. In addition, our spirituality books offer profound guidance for deepening awareness and cultivating healing, self-discovery, and fulfillment.

Founded by psychologist Matthew McKay and Patrick Fanning, New Harbinger is proud to be an independent, employee-owned company. Our books reflect our core values of integrity, innovation, commitment, sustainability, compassion, and trust. Written by leaders in the field and recommended by therapists worldwide, New Harbinger books are practical, accessible, and provide real tools for real change.

🌿 new**harbinger**publications

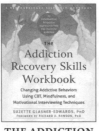
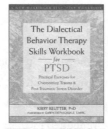
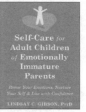